REMY DE GOURMONT (185… important literary critic of his er… authors involved in the Symbolist… them collected in *Le Livre des ma…*  *Deuxième livre des masques* (1898), provided an invaluable map of its extent and a commentary on its ambitions. He became the principal theorist of Symbolism and Decadence, which he regarded as identical. He was one of the founders of the *Mercure de France* and its most prolific contributor, developing his distinctively mannered short fiction in its pages. He collaborated with Alfred Jarry in 1893-94 on *L'Ymagier*, a periodical devoted to Symbolist art extensively trailed in the *Mercure*, which developed a theory of archetypes similar in many respect to Carl Jung's. Disfigured by lupus, he became a recluse before the century ended, and his health deteriorated steadily thereafter, although he kept on writing relentlessly while he could.

BRIAN STABLEFORD has been publishing fiction and non-fiction for fifty years. His fiction includes an eighteen-volume series of "tales of the biotech revolution" and a series of half a dozen metaphysical fantasies set in Paris in the 1840s, featuring Edgar Poe's Auguste Dupin. His most recent non-fiction projects are *New Atlantis: A Narrative History of British Scientific Romance* (Wildside Press, 2016) and *The Plurality of Imaginary Worlds: The Evolution of French* roman scientifique (Black Coat Press, 2016); in association with the latter he has translated approximately a hundred and fifty volumes of texts not previously available in English, similarly issued by Black Coat Press.

REMY DE GOURMONT

From a Faraway Land

TRANSLATED AND WITH AN INTRODUCTION BY
BRIAN STABLEFORD

THIS IS A SNUGGLY BOOK

Translation and Introduction Copyright © 2019
by Brian Stableford.
All rights reserved.

ISBN: 978-1-64525-002-9

Contents

Introduction / 7

Prologue: From a Faraway Land / 25

Part One: Miracles
Phocas / 35
The Metamorphosis of Diana / 44
Regelinde / 50
The Ineffable Will / 56
Hamadryas / 63
The Revolt of the Plebs / 69
The Royal Accident / 79
The Queen's Hands / 84
The Cowshed / 89
The City of the Sphinxes / 96

Part Two: Women's Faces
Irmine / 105
Phenice / 110
Floriberte / 115
Rosule / 120

The Woman in Black / 125
Intact / 130
The Pensive Lady / 136
Melibea / 141
The Virgin of the Plaster Casts / 146
A Virgin's Adventure / 153
Tristane / 159

Part Three: Anecdotes
The Bad Monk / 165
The Evocateur / 170
Jose and Josette / 175
The Man who has Killed / 180
The Last Hour / 185
Emerence / 190
The Burned Château / 197
The Collector / 202
The End of the Walk / 207
The Innocent Siren / 213
Dialogue Between Harvede and a Shade / 218

Introduction

D'UN PAYS LOINTAIN by Remy de Gourmont, here translated as *From a Faraway Land*, was published by the *Mercure de France* in 1898, most of the stories contained therein having appeared in the periodical between 1892 and 1894. It followed a similar collection, *Histoires magiques* (1894; tr. as "Studies in Fascination" in *The Angels of Perversity*) published in the same year as a collection of prose poetry, *Proses moroses*, which assembled many of Gourmont's previous items of fictional prose published in the periodical.

Gourmont was one of the founders of the *Mercure* in 1890, and he was one of its most frequent early contributors. The periodical was explicitly affiliated to the Symbolist Movement in its early years, and the essays and reviews that took up the bulk of its pages made a very considerable contribution to mapping the field of Symbolist literature and art, and promoting its virtues. Initially, it only had 32 pages, a count that rose to 64 at the beginning of 1891, and that space restriction meant that priority had to be given to poetry with regard to creative material. From the very beginning, however, it featured a good deal of prose poetry, in the tradition popularized forty years earlier by Aloysius Bertrand and Charles Baudelaire and subsequently hailed by Joris-Karl Huysmans as "the osmazome [i.e, the essential oil] of literature." Crucial contributions to the magazine made in its first few years by Gourmont, Saint-Pol Roux and Jules Renard all belonged to that lapidary tradition, and many of the other contributors followed the examples they set.

When the *Mercure*'s editor, Alfred Vallette, was able to increase the page-count again, to 96 in 1893 and 128 in 1895, he was progressively able to find room for longer stories, but by then, several of his frequent contributors, including Gourmont, Renard and Gaston Danville had become intensely interested in expanding the scope of prose poetry beyond the lyrical, enhancing its narrative component. That interest complemented a trend that had begun in French newspapers, which elected in the 1880s to feature a good deal short fiction similar in length to the "feuilleton slots" in which they had long been serializing long novels: a space beneath a line ruled near the foot of a page that typically contained between 1400 and 1700 words. Short stories of that approximate length thus become an important market for the writers of the *fin-de-siècle*, and their mass-production, pioneered by Catulle Mendès and taken up with verve by such writers as Octave Mirbeau (the dedicatee of the first story in the "Miracles" section of *D'un pays lointain*), Jules Richepin, Léon Bloy, Marcel Schwob, Edmond Haraucourt, Paul Adam, Jean Lorrain, Bernard Lazare and Jane de La Vaudère, became an important feature of the literary scene of the 1890s. The chief Symbolist periodicals, including the *Revue Blanche*, and *La Vogue*, as well as the *Mercure*, routinely featured fiction of a similar length, which took aboard the narrative techniques and strategies developed by the suppliers of newspaper fiction and hybridized it with the techniques and strategies of Baudelairean prose poetry. Few writers accomplished that hybridization as seamlessly and as elegantly as Gourmont, and if the stories collected in *Histoires magiques* represented his experimental phrase, those in *D'un pay lointain* represent the next phase in that particular literary development, more relaxed, more methodical and arguably more accomplished.

Writers of that kind of short fiction inevitably found it convenient to formulate stories as "character sketches," in which a brief biography of the protagonist was supplemented by a revealing anecdote—a "slice of life" that encapsulated the personality of the individual—usually concluding with an ironic summation of some kind, often assimilating the stories to the genre of *contes cruels*. Gourmont was no exception to that general rule, but he applied that method with a distinctive stylistic elegance, and a particular notion of the inherent "cruelty" of existence that was both subtler and more pointed than the notions possessed by most of his rivals. He was by no means as savage in his dissections as nakedly misanthropic writers like Mirbeau and Bloy, and his relative delicacy and mildness embodies disappointment rather than wrath in its contemplation of the human condition; although he developed that sensibility more elaborately and loquaciously in his novels, the stories in *D'un pays lointain* are assisted by their brevity in making it precise and punctual.

The theory of Symbolism as a literary method, as it was understood in the *fin-de-siècle*, was initially developed by Stéphane Mallarmé and spread via his famous *mardis*, before being expanded and sophisticated by subsequent theorists, most importantly Charles Morice and Gourmont, while other adherents inevitably developed their own philosophies and exemplified it in their works. Gourmont remained something of a purist, however, and maintained a particular affiliation to one point of Mallarmé's program that many others found inconvenient. Mallarmé had proposed that it was essential for Symbolist procedure always to leave something inexplicit and uncertain: an essential ambivalence inherent in the substitution of the symbol for the phenomenon, reflective of the awareness that any interpretative specification is necessarily a falsification. Of all Mallarmé's followers, none took that principle so much to heart as Gourmont, who summarized and exemplified his response to Mallarmé's ideas in the *nouvelle* "Le Pèlerin du silence" [The Pilgrim of Silence] (1890 in the *Mercure de France*) and went on to apply them and develop further exemplifications, becoming a master of understatement. Nowhere in his work is that particular mastery more clearly evidenced than in the short fiction collected in *D'un pays lointain*, for the simple reason that while the prolixity of longer works does not lend itself to understatement, the compact nature of ultra-short stories cries out for it.

That is not to say that all writers—or even very many—creators of such short stories deal in sophisticated understatement; the great majority of *contes cruels* are relatively brutal in their use of "punch lines." Gourmont, by contrast, is a conspicuous exception; no one else pulls their punch-lines as cleverly and as deftly as he does. While shunning brutality, however, the emotional effect is preserved, and perhaps even enhanced; the subtlety and delicacy of his stories does not undermine the quality of their tragedy. No other writer illustrates so well the underrated principle that sometimes, in order to be really cruel, it pays to be gentle. Remy de Gourmont is not a writer who rewards simplistic reading, and readers in search of literary brutality inevitably find his work wanting, but for sophisticated thinkers and connoisseurs of delicacy, he is unmatchable.

In order to understand the particular quality of the world-view that frames the work in this particular collection more fully, it is necessary to know something of the author's biography, and the specific phase in that life-story in which the stories contained in *Du'un pays lointain* were written. Remy de Gourmont was born in 1858, the scion of an aristocratic family that had suffered a drastic decline in its fortunes due to the depredations of the English during the Napoleonic wars. When he was ten years old his family was obliged to leave the Château de la Motte at Bazoches-en-Houlmes, where he had been born, and reside in the far less imposing Manoir de Mesnil-Villeman near Coutances, where he went to school. In 1876 he went to Caen to study law, but moved to Paris the following year, ostensibly to continue his studies there, but actually to devote himself, as he wrote in his diary, to "l'amour et les livres," in order that amour would enable him to develop the sensual aspect of his personality, and books the intellectual aspect.

For Gourmont, that was a typical way of looking at things; he remained permanently preoccupied with notions of personal evolution and self-development, and simultaneously worried by the divisions, tensions and contradictions inherent in the sense of identity. He was perpetually fascinated by dichotomies of all kinds: male and female; thought and emotion; materialism and idealism, etc., and the presumed impossibility of their resolution; for him, the interplay of thesis and antithesis never leads to a satisfactory synthesis. The analyses he carries out in the character studies contained in *D'un pays lointain* are rich in such contrasts, very often transformed into conundrums, the insolubility of which constitutes the fundamental tragedy of human existence.

In 1881 Gourmont obtained a position in the Bibliothèque Nationale, although the pay was scarcely sufficient to meet his living expenses. His early work included the preparation of a series of educational books for young readers, and he began publishing articles in relatively upmarket periodicals, including *Le Monde* and *La Vie Parisienne*. His first novel, *Merlette* (1886) was undistinguished, and the manuscript of a second was lost by the editor to whom it was submitted; there is little hard evidence that his early adventures in amour were as dubiously satisfactory as those early literary endeavors, but even the most superficial reading of his fiction strongly suggests that they must have been. That aspect of his endeavor took a dramatic turn in 1887, however, when he met Berthe Courrière, who features extensively in his early quasi-autobiographical fictions, most obviously in his first successful novel *Sixtine* (1890; tr. as *Very Woman*, 1922) and the novella *Le fantôme* (1891; 1893 in book form; tr. "The Phantom"). The latter offers a jaundiced transfiguration of their affair, but it is not as jaundiced as the more phantasmagorical transfiguration contained in the prologue to the present collection, which seems to have been his last word on the subject.

Berthe Courrière, who was six years older than Gourmont, had aristocratic pretensions, preferring to style herself Berthe de Courrière, although Alfred Vallette's wife and co-editor Rachilde summed up the general opinion of Gourmont's friends by describing her as a "horribly bourgeois fantasist." She also fancied herself a serious student of the occult arts, having thrown herself wholeheartedly into the French Occult Revival; she was closely acquainted with the self-styled Rosicrucian "Sâr" Joséphin Péladan, and with Joris-Karl Huysmans, whose explorations of the Parisian occult demi-monde, incorporated into his classic novel of contemporary Satanism *Là-Bas* (1891), she had assisted. She introduced Gourmont to Huysmans and assisted in the widening of his social horizons that also enabled him to form a brief friendship with Auguste Villiers de l'Isle Adam, one of the great practitioners of the *conte cruel*. The love affair did not last long, but

13

it had a lasting impact, particularly in stripping away many of Gourmont's romantic illusions, and the deep disillusionment that he suffered in its aftermath was probably intensified by Villiers' death in 1889 and the disintegration of his friendship with Huysmans—one of several important literary friendships that were shattered by philosophical differences of opinion, which Gourmont always seems to have taken to heart.

Gourmont was presumably well aware of the mercurial nature of sexual fulfillment, and the extreme difficulty of making the most of it, even before he met Berthe Courrière, but the disenchantment following that infatuation certainly rammed the lesson home. In a kinder world, he might have been able to move on to form new and more satisfactory relationships, but that soon became, at least in his perception, impossible, because from 1891 onwards he suffered progressively from a disease known at the time as "tubercular lupus". As that name implies, it was then widely assumed to be a species of tuberculosis, a disease rife in *fin-de-siècle* Paris with a rich literary legendry. It is now known as "discoid lupus erythematosus" and is thought to be caused by a virus. It is not fatal, nor even particularly debilitating in cases in which it does not develop into "systemic lupus erythematosus," which affects the other organs of the body, but it can be horribly disfiguring. Initially, Gourmont's infection only affected his face, but did so to such an extent that it rapidly became the dominating fact of his life, and he became a recluse. Sympathetic friends continued to visit him, but he became extremely reluctant to go out into a world where he occasioned horror, likely to be refused service even in restaurants that he had previously patronized regularly.

As a result of his disfiguration, Gourmont became a virtual refugee in the world of his own imagination. Arthur Ransome's English translation of *Un Nuit au Luxembourg* (1907), *A Night in the Luxembourg*, is introduced by a memoir in which he records that he found Gourmont, towards the end of his life, living on the fourth floor of a house in the Rue des Saints-Pères, clad in a monastic robe and a grey felt cap, invariably placing his visitors on the far side of his huge desk, with the light directed at their faces, away from his own, carefully keeping his hand in front of his face. Having lost his position at the Bibliothèque Nationale, Gourmont had no alternative but to make his living entirely with his pen, and he set out to do so very methodically, producing essays for periodicals in great profusion—enough, eventually, to fill some fifty volumes, on a wide range of subjects, most importantly a classic study of mysticism and symbolism in Medieval poetry, *Le Latin mystique* (1892), his first two collections of literary criticism, *Le Livre des masques* (1896) and *Le Deuxième livre des masques* (1898), the philosophical essays on esthetics *Le Culture des idées* (1900) and *Le Problème du style* (1902) and a remarkable account of the natural history of sexuality, *Physique de l'amour: Essai sur l'instinct sexuel* (1903; tr. as *The Natural Philosophy of Love*, 1922). Along the way he assisted greatly in the interpretation and popularization of the philosophical ideas of Arthur Schopenhauer and Friedrich Nietzsche, and made a significant contribution to the development of aesthetic philosophy.

All of that work partakes of the world-view that Gourmont formed in the course of, and as a result of, his disillusioned withdrawal into reclusivity. It is not surprising that his first collection of prose poetry was entitled *Proses moroses,* or that the collection of slightly longer stories that he published in between *Histoires magiques* and *D'un pays lointain* was headed by *Le Pèlerin du silence* (1896). It is arguable, however, that the stories collected in *D'un pays lointain* embody the clearest expression of the sentiment of the three years in which that gradual withdrawal took place, eventually becoming complete. They are the quintessential embodiment not only of his burgeoning despair but of the remarkable obliquity and determined courage of his response to it. He was painfully aware that his quest to develop the amorous aspect of his personality was over, but also conscious of the fact that the development of his intellect could not only continue, relatively unhindered, but might even be enhanced, to a certain degree, by his isolation and the obligation to write and publish relentlessly while he died slowly—which he eventually did in 1915.

Gourmont's journey into solitude, although forced upon him, was a bold and determined one, and he carried numerous instruments for the amelioration of his condition in his luggage. He cut himself off from his religious heritage as well as his social heritage, embracing a pugnacious kind of atheism that rejoiced in its own heresy, and also rejected the aspects of contemporary philosophy that seemed to him to have no utility for someone like him, while talking up those that seemed to offer him a valuable pride, if not a viable hope. He took what satisfaction he could from being a unique individual, a man apart in every possible way, demanding respect with an ironically seigneurial hauteur. He earned that respect with the quality of his scholarship and the idiosyncrasy of his outlook. He became the leading literary critic of his day, not merely by virtue of the breadth of his reading and the penetration of his intelligence, but also because he had a unique sympathy with many of the writers whose reputations he helped to establish and secure. He understood better than any other commentator the profound feelings of disenchantment, cynicism and alienation that the writers of the *fin de siècle* had inherited from Baudelaire, and had elevated as bloody banners of their own triumphant distress.

The stories in *D'un pays lointain*, seen as a sketch-map of that intellectual progress, as an exemplification of a descent into despair and a reaction against it, are primarily remarkable for their laconism. That is, in large measure, a consequence of Gourmont's adherence to Mallarmé's literary theory, and his understanding of the manner in which prose poetry and prose fiction could and ought to tackle such a sensibility, but it is also evidence of a mental and philosophical resilience, which finds a peculiar virtue and heroism in resignation and calculated perversity. The analysis and celebration of perversity—especially, but not exclusively, sexual perversity—was the chief stock-in-trade of many of the writers of the *fin-de-siècle*, but the stance adopted by most such writers, whether it was sympathetic or antipathetic, was primarily voyeuristic, distanced by horror, lubricity or a curious combination of both. That is not the case with Gourmont, whose distancing is far more clinical, refusing to deal in shock or surprise, but tacitly counseling and explicitly practicing wry resignation.

The stories themselves are, therefore, the best commentary on what lies behind and beneath them, and Gourmont never commented explicitly on his own work, in which the underexplained is so intrinsic that any explanation would qualify as a betrayal. He did, however, comment freely on the works of other writers, and sometimes saw in them what he must have felt to be echoes of his own psychology and methodology. In *Le Deuxième livre des masques* (1898), for instance, he commented that:

"Some men are not in harmony with their time; they never live with the life of the people; the soul of crowds does not seem to them very superior to the soul of herds. If one of these men reflects on himself and comes to understand himself and to place himself in the vast world, he may grow sad, for about him he feels an invincible stretch of indifference, a mute Nature, stupid stones, geometrical movements; a great social solitude. And from the depths of his ennui he thinks of the simple pleasure of being in harmony, of laughing naturally, of smiling in an unreserved way, of being moved by long commotions. But there may come to him a pride in his renunciation and his isolation, whether he has adopted the pose of a pillar-hermit or whether he has shut the gates of a palace on his pleasures."[1]

The prologue of *D'un pays lointain*, which contains a prospectus of sorts for the collection, makes exactly the same point, albeit much more flamboyantly and dramatically, employing symbolism in its most extreme form, that of allegory. The stories themselves—even those entitled "Miracles"—do not go that far, and their symbolism is often so subdued that it could escape the notice of a casual reader, but the fundamental subtext remains the same: that there is a dignity in loneliness and difference that, without being enviable, is deserving of respect and sympathetic understanding.

This translation was made from the copy of the sixth edition of the text (published in 1922) reproduced on the Bibliothèque Nationale's *gallica* website

—Brian Stableford

---

[1] *Remy de Gourmont: Selections from All His Works Chosen and Translated by Richard Aldington* New York; Covici-Friede, 1929. p.361-2. The word that Aldington translates as "pillar-hermit" is "stylite," which I have transposed directly in the following text, partly because it sounds better and partly because the implicit double meaning of the word "style" is not irrelevant.

From a Faraway Land

Prologue

From a Faraway Land

"WHERE do you come from?"
"From a faraway land. I was born in a black house that surged forth in the middle of a gray plain, around which a circle of light sparkled, like the glories in which the severe features of a stained-glass virgin are inscribed; but that halo of hope and benediction only ringed nothingness, gray and black. My father and mother, like all the inhabitants of that faraway land, were blind; only a few children could see; if that was perceived, their eyes were put out, in order to make them conform. I had a brother whose eyes were put out; I had a sister whose eyes were put out.

"During the operation, carried out by an excellent priest, loved by all and especially the Lord, my mother said: 'It's a brief moment to pass, my dears; I was subjected to it as well, at your age, and I haven't died of it. Come on, have a little courage!' She promised jam, sugar and orange-blossom cakes.

"My father, who was born blind, spoke at greater length. With a rude tenderness he said: 'Little savages, have you no sentiment of propriety? These scamps want to distinguish themselves! These scamps don't want to be like everyone else! You consent, then, to be ridiculous—which is to say, to experience sensation, and hence sentiments or ideas, unknown to humans, and in consequence scorned? Reflect carefully. If you keep your eyes, that incongruous source—so it's said—of vain thoughts and dangerous desires, people will elbow you aside with disdain, they will stamp on your feet, they will knee you in the groin, by mistake; they will gang up on you, they will pull your hair and they will dance a saraband around the curious beast. Oh, you're preparing a fine existence for yourselves!'

"'But they're not refusing to have their eyes put out,' said my mother, 'are you, my dears?'

"'They're not refusing? I should hope not—but I ought to tell them what they'll gain by losing the most despicable of senses and what they'd lose by conserving it. My children, I can list for you, with my double authority of a blind man and a father, the joys of being deprived of sight. The first joy is an intimate and profoundly satisfactory joy, the joy of repulsion overcome, of duty accomplished. Secondly, you'll feel a pleasure of pride, but permissible pride, the pleasure of being absolutely similar to all your little comrades, the pleasure of living among equals. That pleasure will accompany you throughout your life. Finally, castrated of sight, you'll have conquered the peace that is born of incuriosity; after calm games, mild studies, placid amours, good meals and propitious digestions, you'll go to sleep in the certainty of never having strayed from the straight path, never having picked a flower, never having contemplated the sky, or the night when—so it's said—it is ornamented with the saddened gaze of seraphim, or the day, when the Sun, that abominable master of blood and sap, heats up the impurity of instincts . . .'

"My mother interrupted him again: 'How do you expect the children to comprehend such thoughts, my friend? Put yourself within their range. And then, all that is dangerous. By talking like that you're teaching them to reason . . .'

"'Yes, my friend,' said my father, 'that might, perhaps, teach them to reason. Sometimes, an excessively precise knowledge of the good pushes curiosity to turn the page—an action that necessarily produces the greatest misfortunes. So I'll shut up.'

"The excellent priest smiled and contented himself with nodding his head, for he no longer had enough intelligence to speak himself. Outside of his formulas and operations, the old magician was only capable of the words and movements dictated by the instinct of self-preservation. Even his ritual memory was beginning to weaken; he forgot essential words in the pronunciation of exorcisms, and when he remitted the sin—very rare, it's true, in that land—of 'intellectual endeavor' or 'effort to comprehend,' he sometimes failed to demand from the penitent, after the absolution, the sacramental oath: '*Serviam*: I am the eternal slave.'

"Even carried out by debilitated hands, the operation succeeded. My brother and my sister have remained out there in the faraway land."

"But you?"

"I was intelligent and hypocritical. No one ever suspected that I could see. I sealed my impressions, my joys and my desires with a triple lock, in my skull, an invincible strongbox, and one day . . ."

"And one day . . . ?"

". . . I ran away. I traversed the gray plain and, after marching for a long time, I entered a luminous forest, every tree of which resembled a woman with her hair ornamented with diamonds and her neck imaged with pearls. In that forest one respired an air so violently impregnated with odors of life that it gave me a headache; my fingers clenched at the tickling of long grass; my heart sang so forcefully that my entire body trembled. Finally, I held out my hands, embracing, like Apollo, the knees of one of the tree-women. That contact calmed me, but I fell on my side and went to sleep.

"The next day, I continued my journey and I arrived here. At first, I scarcely perceived that I had changed country; the people had open eyes, it's true, but they only seemed to make use of their sight to guide them materially through life. Since then, I've encountered a few veritably sighted individuals.

"I forgot to tell you that while traversing the luminous forest I collected . . . guess what?"

"A rare flower."

"Yes, a soul. In the morning, before quitting the sacred forest that had sheltered my lassitude and prolonged my slumber, I strolled for a little while under the dangling branches, but they were all higher than my raised arm, and I despaired of carrying away even the memory of a leaf. O foliage, which was as alive and as perfumed for me as amorous tresses, I gazed at you undulating above my head, as far from my hand as the wing of a word or the violet snow of early morning clouds. A force drew me and I was about to obey and go away alone, without the witness that I wanted; I was already on the edge and I could see the vast horizon, and in the distance, where the two circles join, the obscure summit of another forest, when a branch flowery with little pink hearts lowered itself toward me, as a gesture of pity. I collected the branch on which the cluster of little pink hearts was trembling, and I continued my route.

"Having arrived at the goal of my journey, I chose a house in order to shelter the flowery branch, as its sisters had sheltered me, for I have always loved the culture of sentiment; it's an occupation full of grace, which only requires the good will of a careful gardener; in the middle of the garden there's a spring where one can wash one's fingers when they're stained with blood.

"So I placed my branch, flowery with little pink hearts, in a majolica vase full of golden sand, and put the vase on a mantelpiece, a primitive altar. To the left of the vase I inclined Filiger's *Les Damnées*,[1] to remind me of the malevolence of the gods, and to the right *La*

---

1 Charles Filiger (1863-1928) was a Symbolist mystic painter, although André Breton hailed him as a pioneering Surrealist. An associate of Paul Gauguin, after the latter left Paris in 1895 he became an alcoholic and an etheromaniac; he would surely have been interned as a lunatic had his family not cared for him scrupulously.

Vigne abandonnée, in which Groux has inscribed the futility of the Sacrifice.[1]

"Then I went to study the forms of life, to learn the manner in which the people of my time laughed, became bored or wept. Most of all they became bored, their passionate capacity being very mediocre and their nervous energy so fugitive that a desire or a dream was often sufficient to exhaust it entirely. I also observed that they became bored without dignity, with the little moans of a chained dog and vain anger against the shrewd and the strong, whose enjoyments irritated their primal impotence. Their consolation was thinking about the future, predicting better times, wallowing in future joys and gazing at the moon with colored lenses.

"I was weary of so many inoffensive stupidities when I encountered Armelle, a vase more beautiful than my majolica vase, from which a golden flower ocellated with blue emerged. She was a creature as stupid as a bird, and as timid, but who allowed herself to be taken in hand. She had no notion of good or evil, nor of beauty or ugliness, an entirely animal sensibility devoid of modesty and disturbance in amour.

---

1 The Belgian Symbolist Henry de Groux (1866-1930) had made a name for himself in Paris before the present story was written with a painting of Christ attacked by a mob; the lithograph cited by Gourmont was produced in association with it. Groux befriended many writers, in addition to Gourmont, in *fin-de-siècle* Paris and was one of Émile Zola's bodyguards in the most critical phase of the Dreyfus Affair. He was reputed to be one of the most extreme of the "Bohemians" of that era and was interned in lunatic asylums more than once.

"At first we had furtive encounters, illusory intimacies, the vanity of which she aggravated by the confession of her regrets and the imploring languor of her attitudes. Deliberately, I prolonged the period of desire; I loved Armelle's impatience and her gesture, on the edge, of wanting to throw herself in the water. Every woman is a virgin for a man who has not possessed her, for virginity is nothing but the unknown, perhaps the most obscure unknown, and I remained on the threshold of the mystery, although its guardian was not at all grim.

"I also desired, by those dilatory games, to exasperate the beast, in order that it would bound in the circus on the day of the fête with savage leaps and all the violence of a nature thwarted and spurred—but I was deceived.

"Having taken her to my house, I explained to her the familiar altar that I had organized with precious decorations around the branch flowering with little pink hearts. My grave and even slightly hieratical attitude astonished her animal candor, accustomed to less solemn prolegomena; she drew nearer and opened wide beautiful blue amorous eyes. The images, severe acolytes, did not capture her gaze; she fixed it without distraction on the branch flowering with little pink hearts. I fell silent, even pretending to devote myself to effacing the dust that troubled one of the corners of the mirror; then her curiosity was emboldened and she touched one of the little pink hearts with her finger; she resembled a cat that wants to play; the whole cluster trembled, and one of the little pink hearts fell into the golden sand. Sure that I had turned my head and forgetful of the mirror, which told me everything, Armelle took the little pink heart and ate it.

"I went to sit down on the far side of the room. Armelle came to me, and I saw her advance, entirely pale with amour; her attitude of a fluttering bird was transformed into the splendid grace of a swan dying on a canal with a royal pride; her movements were scarcely visible under her loose dress, and her arms dangled alongside her body like stems broken by a gust of wind.

"She came to me and knelt down, kissing my hands; then she wept silently. Dolor did not contradict the purity of her ecstatic face and the transparent tears that rolled down her cheeks resembled pearls detached from a chaplet of smiles.

"I leaned over her and I kissed her on the forehead, softly; a few pearls were still falling from her smiling eyes, a few pearls and the cross—and a deep sigh announced that Armelle's heart had been relieved, bead by bead, of the entire rosary of supreme dolors and infinite joys.

"Her body collapsed on my feet, her head stopped on my knees and her arms fell, truly like stems massacred by a storm.

"Armelle was dead.

"I understood that the little pink hearts were marvelous hosts, each containing a soul, and I also understood that by taking communion with one of those little pink hearts, Armelle had poisoned herself. Souls are terrible poisons."

Part One:

Miracles

Phocas

To Octave Mirbeau

THE PRAETOR himself gave the most precise instructions to the decurion charged with arresting Phocas.[1] That magistrate, Aurelius by name, was a serious, honest and intelligent man. A great legal expert, he would not abuse his science, nor statutes, nor edicts to crush with a uniform and traditional rigor the criminals committed to his tribunal. Entirely to the contrary; profiting from the freedom which judges then had to decide according to their conscience, he liked to forget the hardened imperative of the penal laws. More than once he imposed heavy fines on misers and the inflexible rich, guilty, according to him, of not allowing themselves to be robbed, given that the thief was in the more extreme need and that there is a certain degree of poverty that authorizes a man who has nothing to take from one who possesses everything.

---

[1] This story recycles the legend of Saint Phocas the Gardener, who was allegedly martyred during the persecution of Diocletian at the beginning of the fourth century A.D.

Such judgments would seem scandalous today and our refined morality would be indignant in consequence, but in the fourth century, at Sinope, in the province of Pont, where these events came to pass, men denuded of high principles freely accepted the kind of justice that Aurelius understood; annoyed, but fully convinced that letting a human creature die of hunger and strangling him with one's own hands are equal crimes, they paid the fines; then, to avoid further just thefts, they would give to the poor of their own free will.

Christian ideas had penetrated little by little into Sinope, as they had in the greater part of the Roman Empire, but not yet under their true name; that name was still detested, and people there professed for the new religion a horror mingled with dread; but, in advance of its dogmas, the principles of justice and pity had crept like lame beggars over the walls of the town, and murmured singular words that the people repeated with surprise.

Of true Christians, instructed as to the birth, death and resurrection of the Nazarene, there were only a few in Sinope among the weavers of the outlying districts, the peasants of the countryside and the slaves of the great estates. It was rumored that the chief among them—the most fully-instructed and, in consequence, the most dangerous—was a man named Phocas, a gardener by profession, a free man who cultivated a smallholding and sold its produce at the town gate.

Thus, by a strange contradiction, the people of Sinope, who loved justice, hated those who were the living examples of justice. Even Aurelius, the helpful judge, lost his temper and swore by the infernal gods as soon as the name of Christ was pronounced in front of him. Meanwhile, edicts arrived from Rome which commanded the searching out and condemnation of all the followers of the new religion. Aurelius read the edicts that were sent to him by the prefect of the province and, for the first time in his life, was glad to have read an imperial edict.

Having summoned Amasius, the officer in charge of the decury of soldiers employed to search out criminals, Aurelius commanded him to seize Phocas and bring him to Sinope, dead or alive.

The instructions, written on a tablet of wax, were: *Phocas, Christian, scorner of the Gods, enemy of the emperor and the Roman people. Notorious bandit and guileful conspirator, chief of a band of cruel rogues, he is also a very accomplished magician. He knows the mysterious art of killing at a distance, either by frightful combinations of elements, or by signs, or by a secret compact with infernal spirits. You must approach him prudently and cunningly; your life might depend on it, but it will surely be the salvation of the Republic.*

Amasius considered these instructions, chose a few resolute legionaries, veterans of the barbarian wars, and the little troop set forth. They went somewhat at hazard, because, policing being summary in those days, they did not know the exact location where Phocas conspired and watered his salad vegetables. It had to be in the depths of a small valley that hollowed out a clearing of grass in the forest. They went there first, to make enquiries of the woodcutters.

In the imagination of Amasius, a brave decurion who had slain more Goths than he had teeth in his jaws, Phocas was hiding in a shadowy cavern or some other inaccessible lair, and he anticipated that his quest would be difficult and distressing; but the weather was fine and the men determined. *We'll get away with sleeping in the open for a few nights*, he thought, *under the protection of the goddess with the twelve breasts*.[1]

They left early in the morning and, having followed a stream that divided the forest of Sinope in two, they found themselves, a little before midday, facing a small hut covered with roses, which appeared to have a pleasant garden behind it. Amasius saw no cause for suspicion; he knocked at the door and requested hospitality.

The door opened and a man appeared, dressed like a peasant, in a short tunic that left his legs bare below the knees. His hair was short and his beard long. He seemed weary and gentle. His eyes, behind lowered lids, were blue and a little vague.

The man seemed to be about fifty years old, but his soul was certainly young, for he expressed great pleasure at the fact that Providence had brought strangers to his door.

"Come in, come in! What! Soldiers? Have the Goths returned?"

"No," said Amasius, "but we're looking for a bandit more ferocious than the sons of the Amales,[2] a

---

1 i.e. Diana
2 The Amales were one of the "royal families" (or, more prosaically, tribes) of the Ostrogoths; the most famous of the "sons of

Christian, a scorner of the gods"—he was quoting his commission—"a magician who knows the incredible art of killing at a distance . . ."

"There are no magicians around here," Phocas said, "but the country is full of thieves. They don't even wait until my vegetables are grown before they tear them up. They double my labor, requiring me to start planting all over again—but what do you expect? If they take my vegetables from me, it's because they have need of them—perhaps a greater need than mine. I forgive them and I give them what they steal from me."

"You're too indulgent," said Amasius. "The Emperor, who is just, has resolved to punish the chief of these rogues—for it must be their leader to whom my orders refer."

"What is his name?" asked Phocas.

"His name?" Amasius consulted his tablets. "Phocas."

"Phocas!" said the poor gardener. "But I know him—he lives close by. He's a Christian."

"My instructions relate to him," said Amasius.

"It's really him," said Phocas, "a ferocious Christian, a scorner of the gods! I'll take you to him myself, before sunset. You're lucky. Phocas! Don't worry, he'll belong to you; he's in your hands. But in the meantime, since you're my guests, I owe you hospitality, first of all, a meal. Bread, and vegetables from my garden—those that Phocas has left there."

---

the Amales" was Theodoric the Great, the founder of the Gothic kingdom in Italy, which inherited the ruins of the western Roman Empire in the fifth century.

"Is it Phocas who steals your salads?" Amasius asked.

"In person."

"We shan't spare him."

"I certainly hope so," said Phocas. He went on: "And for guests, I keep an amphora of Asian wine buried underground. I never drink it myself, because the water from the stream is so good . . ."

"We'll drink it!" the soldiers said.

"I hope so," said Phocas.

The soldiers and the gardener sat down at the table. Phocas, at the insistence of Amasius, drank a little wine and became a little excited.

"How I love you, my friends," he cried. "You and all my brothers, all men! Often, when I rest from my labor—when my lettuces, watered, fall asleep like good little creatures in the peace of the night—I dream of the future happiness of humankind, the children of God, and also of the immediate happiness that each of us can find within himself, if he lives in love, justice and charity. Love one another. If your brother is cold, give him a place at your hearth. If he is hungry, sit him down at your table. If he is ignorant, instruct him. If he is wicked, strive to be good in being good to him. Times are changing. I see a new age coming, an angel clad all in white like a morning sky; he is coming over the sea, and the waves calm down as he passes, and the great birds that soar over the waters flutter around him, forming a procession of love . . . He is coming; I see him! He has the clear eyes of a messenger bearing good news; he is singing a hymn of joy; the beating of his wings has a calming influence . . . He is coming, I see him! The luminous archangel is landing among us . . . love, love, be implacable by dint of loving! Love men in spite of them, love them so much that your love tames them, transforms them and refashions them in the image of the One who, though all-powerful, chose to die . . ."

The soldiers were moved, although they did not really understand. Amasius would have liked to hear more of that talk of love, which was more intoxicating than the wine of Asia—but, faithful to the word of his command, he thought of Phocas the abominable bandit, and he made the effort to say: "Master, I will come to see you again, for your discourse has moved me as I have never been moved before by the most beautiful speeches. I shall never forget you. I've heard tell of a philosopher called Socrates, or Plato, I no longer remember, whom my centurion venerates like a god . . . You are my Socrates . . . Oh! your words have done me good . . . Never have I heard such things . . ."

He fell silent; then made a new effort: "And this Phocas?"

The poor gardener rose to his feet and said: "I am Phocas."

"You? Master, has the Asian wine made your head spin?"

"I am Phocas."

By means of wax tablets, and a bronze plaque which affirmed the gratitude owed to him by the town of Antioch for his courage in a time of plague, Phocas proved that he was Phocas.

41

Convinced, Amasius murmured some words of contempt for the stupidity of the Praetor Aurelius—and then he took Phocas away. The night was not far advanced when they re-entered Sinope.

※

As soon as the following morning, Phocas was judged. The people, forewarned, gathered in a great crowd. At the sight of the bandit, the Christian, the blasphemer who hated the gods, they let out joyous cries:

"Put him to death! Put him to death!" cried the people.

Aurelius, after some minor tortures and an investigative hearing, during which Phocas had admitted his crime of being a Christian, pronounced his sentence:

"To the beasts!"

And the people repeated: "To the beasts with the Christian! To the beasts, to the beasts!"

Shortly before midday, the circus was opened and Phocas appeared in the arena. Careless of the howling of the happy crowd, without any thought of wild beasts or bulls, he cried in a loud voice: "I am a Christian!"

Then he fell to his knees in prayer, and waited.

It was a bull that came out of the ergastule.

The beast fell upon its quarry, pierced him with a thrust of its horn, threw him into the air, and then moved away.

Phocas fell back amid a rain of blood. He had not even lost consciousness, and, clutching his belly, from which his entrails were emerging, he managed to resume his kneeling position and continued his prayer.

At that moment he perceived, next to the door of the ergastule, Amasius and his soldiers, who had been posted there, swords in hand, in order to chase the victim back to the center of the arena if he sought to flee towards the cellars. He recognized his friends and, gathering his strength, raised himself up in order to send them, with a heavy hand, a sign of love and a sign of farewell.

The soldiers, who had been touched by a desire for glory and mystery, looked at one another for a moment. Then, as one, they leapt forward and ran towards Phocas, crying: "We are the sons of Phocas! We are Christians!"

It was a beautiful fête, which the people of Sinope remembered for a long time, for the lions and the panthers were loosed, and instead of a single victim, there were twelve; the eyes of the women drank the blood.

The Metamorphosis of Diana

WHEN he saw the moon fading and tremulous in the clear sky, like a lost veil afloat on a blue sea, Heliodorus was afraid of such an omen and, standing erect, with his arms upraised, he pronounced the words of conjuration.

It was in vain. The gods fled with deaf ears; and from their lips, once so eloquent and so rich in wisdom, nothing fell any longer in the sanctuary but oracles shattered by invisible thunderbolts of a new kind.

Heliodorus resumed his place on the stone bench at the threshold of the temple. The evening breeze was as sad as an adieu; no other sound could be heard but the sobbing of the reeds. He wept like the reeds, at one with them in mourning things and the gods.

He wept for a long time; then he fell asleep on the threshold, still a guardian and a priest. He was awakened again by loud cries and the light of torches. People were coming towards him, short in stature, half-naked, girded in ill-scraped hides, with long oiled hair, spears in their hands and pine-branches blazing and smoking in the night. The leader brought his spear down upon the head of Heliodorus, and the priest, bound with thongs, was thrown among the sobbing reeds. Then the temple of Diana with the white knees was systematically pillaged.

The barbarians had a destructive power that was truly divine; what men had taken centuries to construct, they demolished in a few hours of night, and when all the stolen gold was loaded on their chariots, they were excited by derision to drag out of the temple the inviolate Artemis, whose marble, by virtue of its supernatural candor, astonished the piety of pilgrims. Then, doubtless wanting to be agreeable to their own god, and believing that they might annihilate her indestructible grace, they tried to smash the effigy of the white goddess; but the effigy remained determinedly intact, and the barbarians went away, weary of a futile sacrilege.

Then Heliodorus broke his bonds, and got to his feet lamentably, amid the sobbing reeds; the new day dawned. Having washed away the mud that blinded his eyes, he looked with horror at the blasphemous devastation and the Virgin, his beloved, laid across the footpath like a cadaver, left there after the murder and the nocturnal stupor.

He let himself fall beside the goddess and, having kissed her feet, lost consciousness.

✵

"Pure marble, graceful marble,

"Proud knees,

"Hips upon which no hand has ever inscribed its desire,

"Cradle in which no infant has ever slept,

"Spring from which no bird has ever come to drink,

"Inaccessible abdomen,

"Eternal snows,

"Arms that have only deigned to embrace the sacred boles of oaks,

"Hands that have only caressed the flanks of white dogs,

"Breasts that had only palpated the agony of hinds,

"Proud mouth,

"Pure marble, graceful marble!"

❋

Heliodorus muttered those litanies in his sleep. To each invocation he added a pardon, a supplication, the expression of his shame, his despair and his love.

"Forgive me, Diana Artemis! You appointed me as your guardian and I was not able to keep thieves away from you! You chose me as your priest and I was not able to preserve you from sacrilege."

When Heliodorus was praying thus, in all simplicity and all humility, it seemed to him that the goddess rose up and leaned towards him, and it seemed to him that her proud and graceful mouth said:

"I forgive you, Heliodorus, for you would have given your life for me, if I had wanted your life; but the barbarians let you live by my command, in order that you might witness a miracle whose like no man has yet seen.

"The gods are ancient, Heliodorus, as you know; but ancient as they are, they were born and they must all die. The hour of their death has come. The gods are dying even as I speak to you, but they are not dying as humans die; they are dying as gods; their essence persists and will live again in new forms.

"These changes are necessary for their own glory and for the joy of humans. When gods are too old they no longer inspire either terror or love. They become indifferent to simple souls and distracted hearts. Humans, those eternal prisoners, no longer have confidence in the ladder of grace, fearful that it might break beneath their feet; they no longer dare to climb heavenwards; then, fallen back into the sadness of their nature, they crawl, as they did in the first days of the world, in the obscure marsh of animality.

"New ladders are necessary; that is why trees have been felled in the forest of infinity.

"Sleep, Heliodorus. When you wake up, you who loved me as I was, will love me as I will be; and by means of the new ladder, you will climb so high that you will have vertigo."

Diana fell silent, and Heliodorus thought that he saw a woman going towards the temple, dressed in a trailing white robe strewn with blue stars. Her head was surrounded by divine light, and soft rays were falling from her extended hands towards the earth. She went into the temple.

❋

Heliodorus slept again. When he awoke, he saw that the temple had been restored in a new artistic style. The whiteness of the walls was covered with paintings of unknown figures, haloes, lambs and symbols like the Greek letter tau.

Heliodorus got up and entered the sanctuary, whose guardian and priest he still believed himself to be. Doubtless befuddled by such a long sleep, he did not recognize the ornaments, vases, lamps and censers that had taken their place of those that had been looted, or the physiognomy of the worshipers, or the sacred effigy that stood eternally erect beneath the same canopy of silk and pearls. He was still standing there, utterly astonished, when the voice of his dream sounded once again in his heart:

"Recognize me, Heliodorus, and love me as you loved Diana. I am the eternal Virgin. Come to me. If you address a few words of love to me, you will understand, for it is love that makes everything understandable. Come, Heliodorus, and set your foot on the first step of the ladder."

The congregation sang:

Ave, semper virgo,
Ave, scala coeli.

Heliodorus mingled his own voice with that of the choir, and immediately perceived, looming up before him, a new ladder made with the most precious wood of all, felled in the forest of infinity. Impulsively, he climbed to the highest rung. He climbed so high that he had vertigo, so high that he understood the eternal mysteries and the nature of the law which decrees that everything changeable only changes in form, and not in essence.

Regelinde

IT was in the times when the providential barbarians arrived to liberate Europe from Roman tradition. The Goths were fecundating slothful Spain. A new beauty sprang forth amid the debris of vain temples: From Aphrodites shattered like the stones once thrown by Deucalion, a new humanity was born into the world, radiant with energy and naïvety, ingenuous and violent, and from the dust of Ceres, ground by heavy millstones accustomed to the docility of grain, the men of the North kneaded an unknown bread, which gave to males the mystery of the will, and to women the mystery of grace.

Regelinde was the daughter of a king: a jewel whose case had been closed upon her on the day of her birth and never re-opened. She lived in the palace and the royal gardens, alone in her rank and alone in her essence, as unique as an amethyst sculpted into a cup, from which her father had only drunk once, mingling with the dark wine the fresh blood of a tributary rebellious to tribute.

Clad in a white robe decorated with a cross of jet, with a crimson collar and the silver ring of a secret betrothal on her finger, she walked in silence. The officers fell silent as she went by and bowed, their eyes veiled by their left hands in the Oriental fashion imported to Hispalis[1] by Isidore, son of Gregory, the king's physician and a learned man.

No one ever spoke to Regelinde except her father, Rescaon, Bishop Majorian, and her nurse Ipa. None of her forty slaves would have dared to touch the hem of her dress without an order from her eyes or a sign from her finger; Regelinde was the daughter of a king: a princess, mutely adored by the people of the palace like an emanation or an incarnation of Iscratene, the boreal Sun, like Iscratene herself, the feminine Star which loves humans for six months and hates them for six months.

But Rescaon was a Christian, baptized in the snows by Abbas the Martyr, who, in order to inundate the child, master of the North, had used the heat of his hand to melt a piece of ice cut in the form of a crescent moon—and Regelinde, a Christian, did not believe in Iscratene, but the privileged daughter of the living God.

Humble at the feet of Bishop Majorian, meekly accepting his penitential speeches, and humble in the face of her father, ears open to his counsel, the princess rediscovered in solitude the pride of being the unique Regelinde and the joy of being loved by the One before

---

[1] Hispalis was the Roman name of the city now known as Seville.

whom kings were only dust and bishops ash. God loved Rescaon; God loved Majorian; God loved Ipa—but God did not love Ipa, Majorian or Rescaon as he loved Regelinde; and that was true, as true as it is that there are seven planets in the firmament, as true as it is that thunder is a clamor of the sky, a warning that we have to weep for our sins.

One morning, Rescaon called his daughter and announced to her the impending arrival of the prince to which she was secretly betrothed. The courier had arrived in the night, preceding him by six days' march. She was instructed to prepare to receive as her lord the young king of Hippona,[1] Saran, who wore on his finger a silver ring exactly similar to Regelinde's ring.

Saran! She had often dreamed about Hippona and Saran; by dint of thinking about him when her nurse told her the story of her secret betrothal, she sometimes even pictured him in her imagination: similar to and as superb as Zinthe, the captain of the blue archers, who had a zigzag of lightning tattooed on his forehead, as superb, with a gaze as coldly mild, but more regal.

Saran! She was, therefore, to become a woman!

Regelinde meditated that mystery, but as she was very pure, it was in vain. Doubtless, the day after the wedding, instead of the white robe starred with the cross of jet, she would don a crimson robe, and when she became a mother, a robe of green fringed with red gold if she bore a son, or flax-blue if she bore a girl—but how would she become a mother?

---

[1] The Roman city of Hippo Regius, which had several other names before becoming the modern Annaba

Interrogated, Ipa raised her gray eyes to the heaves and said: "Iscratene, my mother, Christ, my savior, do you hear what she is asking?"

That was all. Then Regelinde commanded that Isidore, son of Gregory, should be summoned and left alone with her.

As well as being the king's physician and master of ceremonies, Isidore was a magician. He had studied under the most knowledgeable teachers in Thebes, Chrysopolis, Alexandria and, finally, in Erythraea, the city of the red sands, the inhabitants of which conversed freely with demons, and whose prince, Hucar, thrice resuscitated, used up more women in one day than there were clusters of grapes on a royal vine.

Isidore came in. He was neither young nor old, but he appeared full of life, endowed with supernatural health.

"Princess Regelinde, the man with whom you, a virgin, seclude yourself, ought to be an old man."

Isidore collapsed all of a sudden, as if beneath the burden of centuries, and Regelinde spoke.

"Teach me the science of generation. Tell me how the Father engenders the Son; tell me what the conjugations of the stars are. Name the principles, the causes and the means. Who is the father of the fauns, and who is their mother? Teach me the norms and the ambigenies,[1] the genealogy of similarities and that of disparities, the creation of the human and that of the

---

1 This rare Latin term is approximately similar to the modern concept of hybridity, referring to dual parentage.

goat, that of the musimon,[1] and that of the angel. I'm listening."

"I shall say nothing," Isidore, the son of Gregory, replied, "but look."

And the infinity of worlds unfurled in space, like the links of a prodigious chain. Regelinde saw the succession of generations, the desires and the works, the acts of amour and the births.

She saw, at the commencement of things, the shadow of the Father, immense in the pale sky—and of the Father, as a surgeon, the son was produced.

She saw the amorous stars mingle their fluids—and new lights immediately populated the firmament.

She saw the Principle, which is a wheel whose hub is a diamond, whose spokes are the seven primordial stones, and whose rim is a unique alloy of all the pure metals—and she understood that the principle, the cause and the means are One.

She saw the creation of the angel, the brush of wings, the creation of the aegipan,[2] the pan-goat, the faun and the musimon.

She saw, finally, by what means humans receive life—but then the shame was then so strong in her pure heart, and the fear so violent in her chaste soul, that she suspended the mage Isidore's evocative arm, fell to her knees and cried:

---

1 Musimon is an obsolete term for the animal now known as a mouflon, which was once thought to be a hybrid of a sheep and a goat.
2 It is not obvious how aegipans differ from fauns, the name Aegipan probably having originated as an alternative name for the god Pan.

"After having seen that, I do not want to see any more. May those images remain forever beneath my eyelids, and alone, in order to inform me that I ought not to be like other females, and that my pride ought to be different from the pride of all other women and all other beasts. I want to be loved, I want to be fecundated, but only by superior methods, and not according to animal formulas; there is no point, since I possess henceforth the knowledge of the principle, the cause and the means. God, through the intermediary of the Mage, has instructed his daughter spiritually; the flesh is useless to me, and I deny its instincts.

"Saran, I shall not be your wife, for you would despise a beauty self-destroyed."

She removed the silver ring of the secret betrothal from her finger and gave it to Isidore, saying: "You must make me another, adding to that one its weight in gold, in order to signify the union of Regelinde and the Infinite."

Then she said: "Salvation is acting in negation of natural laws."

"That is so," agreed the Mage.

When he had gone, Regelinde put out her eyes.

The Ineffable Will

SER BONDETTO of Florence was a rich man, but not very respectable. He bought cereals at a low price in years when the harvest was good, and sold them dear to improvident people during lean years. In those innocent times—it was the year 1240 or thereabouts—such commerce was reproved and those who speculated on the confidence of the humble and the weak, growing rich in the bread of the poor, were scorned. More than once, to universal applause, the exasperated populace looted his warehouses and smashed his coffers, but Ser Bondetto had hidden reserves, cellars as profound as catacombs, where gold and wheat, the strength and the soul of the world, lay dormant, and after every riot he was still as rich and as powerful as he was wicked.

His wife Bonadonna co-operated in his evil work; she kept the register of sales and purchases, and she weighed the pieces of gold in a little set of uncommonly wise scales, which knew how to tip at exactly the right moment, and which had enriched its masters on its own. Bonadonna's gestures were exquisite and precious: her little finger settled, with the lightness and celerity of a bird, on one pan or the other and corrected, with an invisible dexterity, the inflexibility of justice. She was very charming in that role and Ser Bondetto loved her very much; in the evening, when they made up their accounts, they resembled a painting that is in the Louvre, for, while her husband checked the calculations and thefts of his cherished companion, Bonadonna opened a Book of Hours, enlivened by vivid miniatures, and read mild prayers aloud.

They prospered, therefore, in spite of the rancor and violence of the people, and they were happy, living in joy and labor, augmenting their fortune without neglecting their salvation.

To tell the truth, they understood no better than their modern brethren that they were rogues; their wickedness was entirely instinctive and they had never assessed their villainy in rational terms. If humans could assess their villainy rationally, they would no longer be villains.

Like good Christians they went to Church at the appointed times, and added to their account many works of supererogation. Miserly for the poor, they were generous for the clergy, and the clergy esteemed them.

Now, it happened that a singular preacher came to Florence, and from the first day made himself heard there. He was poorly clad, like a beggar and he spoke to the people in a strong, clear voice, no matter where, in the squares, at crossroads, in the courtyards of hostelries. As to what he said, nothing like it had ever been heard before. He did not quote Latin, he did not use eloquent phrases, he did not organize long and sonorous sentences, he did not divide his discourse into several points, he made no use of personification, irony, exordium or peroration; he simply said: "Love one another, and in order to love better, make yourselves poor, for one only loves well when one is liberated from the wealth that hardens the heart and renders it as inert as a gold coin; and if you are already poor rejoices, for you are Christ's chosen, and the true princes of his empire. Woe to the rich! They have been found loveless, and they have been damned."

He said these things, and many others, and souls were touched, and the priests, who were among the rich, were afraid. In order that the pauper should not seem to be preaching against them, they opened their churches to him and offered their pulpits to him, although he had not received holy orders, and was only a man of good will.

He preached one evening in the church of Saint Como, which was Ser Bondetto's parish; he took care to be there, in the front row, with his dear Bonadonna, and they both listened, entranced and astonished, to truths of which they were ignorant.

On returning to their lodgings, escorted by servants carrying torches, they did not dare, contrary to their habit, to share their impressions. This time, they were too violent, and above all too novel; it was as if they were intoxicated by them.

The following morning, the first customer who entered the shop was an old man. He had come to ask for a pennyworth of wheat.

"Why do you want a pennyworth of wheat?" asked Ser Bondetto. "What can one do with a pennyworth of wheat? In any case, I don't sell such small quantities. I sell to the millers, the millers sell to the bakers, and the bakers sell to the people. Here, therefore, is a ducat; buy bread, wine, olives, and be happy."

"Do you know that old man, Ser Bondetto?" asked Bonadonna, when the poor man had gone. "Myself, I've never seen him before."

"No more have I, Bonadonna. I have never seen him; he is undoubtedly not from Florence."

"Perhaps he has come a long way."

"Perhaps," said Bondetto.

"You've done well to give him a ducat," said Bonadonna.

"I gave it to him without thinking," said Bondetto.

"You've done well, Ser Bondetto," repeated Bonadonna, "for I believe that poor man has been sent by Christ, in order to test our hearts."

"That is my opinion too," Bondetto replied.

From that day on, Bonadonna renounced the delicate movements of her little finger, as light as a bird, and the millers of Florence were surprised by the unusual generosity of Ser Bondetto, who now, for a measure, voluntarily delivered a measure and a half. Everyone hastened towards his shop, all eager to profit from what they believed to be a temporary aberration, for they all wanted to profit from it, all wanting to die rich, in accordance with the motto which has become, with the passage of time, the motto of all civilized men.

In the meantime, Ser Bondetto sold all his wheat, and as he had neglected to buy more, having other ideas, he closed his shop and said to Bonadonna: "I have no more corn and my coffers are full of gold. What will we do with so much gold? Don't you think that it would be appropriate to give it to the poor, if they want it?"

"I think so," said Bonadonna. "Only keep back sufficient to buy a little house, a field, a carriage and a donkey, because I want to retire to the countryside."

It was done in accordance with Bonadonna's wishes. Retiring to a meager hut, they became gardeners and they lived by the labor of their hands. Having become poor, although their youth was long past, they felt suddenly rejuvenated, like a half-dead tree spared from the gluttony of its large and heavy branches by their amputation. The love that they had lavished on their wheat, their gold, their silver vessels, their silken clothes, their sculpted furniture and their jewels—the love that had been exteriorized toward the fornication of metal and wood—re-entered into their hearts, and they began to love one another more and more; the archangels and the seraphim were scarcely capable of such profound devotion.

They loved one another in God, by virtue of their renunciation. Possessing nothing more than was necessary, they had everything and more: all the spiritual riches disdained by those who adored nothing but material wealth.

They loved one another and were no longer able to talk; spending entire days stooped over the soil, they plied their spades in silence, content and calm to look at one another secretly, in the knowledge that they were bound together in a community of love and work.

However, no longer being egotists, the love that they had for one another was no longer sufficient and they set about loving their neighbors, and then all humans, particularly those who were the poorest of all: those who travelled the roads without bread, or water to drink, devoid of hope and joy; they welcomed them to their little house, even running along the road to meet them; in order to feed them, they worked twice as hard, but those they had helped were not ungrateful, and helped them in their labor, and the miserable abode of Ser Bondetto became a little colony of humbly happy people.

After twenty years of perfect life, Bonadonna, having reserved too little of her strength, fell ill and was soon at the point of death, at the page of the book that would have been the sweetest all—for her hope was infinite—if Ser Bondetto had been able to read it, leaning over her, his head against hers. Ser Bondetto was, however, in good health; although his best days were long gone, his strength had not yet begun to fail. He too was desolate, however. He saw, with woebegone eyes, the advent of the Liberator who was not coming for him, and he often wept because he was not dying.

The ultimate hour arrived, when Bonadonna asked for the last rites. Ser Bondetto went to fetch a priest.

The holy oil had no sooner touched the forehead of the dying woman, and the friends of the family had no sooner concluded their prayers of mourning, than Bondetto, who was weeping on his knees, got up and said: "I wish to die too!"

And, lying down beside his wife, whose hand he seized, he received, after her, the consolation of the holy oil and the grace of the last sacrament.

Afterwards, as the amazed helpers fell silent and watched, admiring that incredible miracle of love and will, Ser Bondetto and Bonadonna uttered a long moan in unison.

They were dead.

Hamadryas

MARQUISE FIORAVANTI received the elegant mythological nickname of Hamadryas upon her entry into the Academy of Asolans, where Cardinal Bembo delighted beautiful and noble ladies and learned cavaliers with amorous casuistries.[1] Meetings of the Academy were held at the cardinal's villa, situated beneath pines and oaks. There, they discussed all the cases of conscience that might concern lovers who were no less masters of their senses than their hearts, after the fashion of the peripatetic philosophers.

Bembo, smiling gravely, often had the last word, and he would lift his head with satisfaction, shaking the red tassels that hung from his white felt hat. Sometimes, however, the cavaliers also discovered serious arguments while recalling their adventures, and the princesses and marquises, although inclined to irony,

---

[1] Pietro Bembo (1470-1547) was an important linguistic scholar, whose *Gli Asolani* (1505), after which the fictitious "academy" featured here is named, is a series of dialogues on the subject of Platonic amour, dedicated to Lucrezia Borgia, with whom he had a notorious affair.

would often find ingenious resolutions to questions of principle that perplexed the cardinal and rendered the priests thoughtful.

Thus, the question was posed:

"If a woman is loved by a timid admirer, how far may she encourage the admirer in question by giving him unequivocal evidence of her solicitude? For example, might she openly seek out his company, ask for his hand to assist her in descending a staircase, compliment him on his figure, or even go so far as to kiss him?"

The controversy regarding that particular question went straight to the kiss, and extended at some length. Women, refined and committed egotists, praised the charm of being loved by a man so discreet that he spoke with his eyes alone. There was, they said, an exquisite pleasure to be derived from the mute adoration and painful constraint of a creature so devoted as to be enslaved. The kiss would spoil everything, because it would transform timidity into audacity, and it would soon become necessary to surrender on all fronts at once, abandoning to the victor what he should have conquered for himself, all the redoubts, and the stronghold.

"The Castel Sant'Angelo!" ventured one cavalier, whose manner of speaking was light but bold.

That description brought a smile from the cardinal, then a merry laugh. Encouraged by that condescension, the princesses and marquises repeated the pretty metaphor in a slightly scandalized tone.

"Sire," said Hamadryas, who had not yet spoken or laughed that day, "your description is one of the most beautiful to have emerged from our Academy. Together with the fame that will be attached in future centuries to the name of our cardinal, if I am not mistaken, it will surely secure our eternal renown. The Castel Sant'Angelo is the key to Rome, to the extent that whoever holds that fortress is master of the city. It is the same with a woman: once master of the castle, you are master of all the palaces, all the pleasures, thoughts, desires and dreams that bestir agreeable forms in that little world. Whether you take it by connivance, trickery or force, the result is always the same and the submission as absolute."

"That's going too fast, Madame," said the cardinal, "and you're settling questions of the utmost subtlety very violently."

The marquises and the princesses said, ingenuously: "Madame, you have betrayed us."

※

Hamadryas never returned to the shadow of the pines and the oaks to dispute with the Asolans. She found them puerile and rather hypocritical. In joining their company she had believed that frank and honest discussions might permit her to revive, elegantly, the amorous pleasures to which wearily she had just bid adieu, in spite of having scarcely turned thirty. But the distinctions of those cold souls, light hearts and fashionably perverted spirits exasperated her, and also humiliated her. She had lived so much and loved so abundantly that the cerebral debauches of those prudent individuals seemed to be the dreams of sick children, and the cardinal, whom she held nevertheless in esteem, appeared to her to be a naïve and complicated pedagogue, probably impotent, and slightly ridiculous.

Having thus abandoned the Asolans, she wished to purify herself in action, and to wash away, with kisses that were not at all metaphorical, the Platonic blue with which she felt that her skin had been tinted. So she abandoned herself to love for the hundredth time, with all the pagan sensuality she could muster, all that remained to her of faith and disinterest.

But the viol no longer vibrated.

Then, she considered her beauty and wanted it to be immortal.

Her beauty, her body, her figure: in sum, she had never loved anything else. And on returning from each of her voyages in search of love, with what joy, taking possession of herself again, she rediscovered the absolute grace of her adored flesh!

Michelangelo had sculpted his own glorious Hamadryas in marble, and Marquise Fioravanti exhibited in her palace, in the festival gallery, among the fountains of agate and gods of bronze, the unparalleled masterpiece of her own beauty. Her pedestal bore the inscription of her one and only name, Hamadryas, in order that posterity might revere like a goddess the woman who desired nothing but the anonymous glory of having been beautiful.

And the cardinals, the priests, the cavaliers, the princesses and the marquises passed through the gallery of the Fioravanti Palace, admiring the work of the sculptor even and criticizing the shamelessness of Hamadryas. She was there, listening to their remarks, enjoying their envy, pleasant and proud, wanting, for her supreme moment, to leave the memory of a uniquely imperious grace.

Then, when everyone had departed, to the sound of violins and harps, she lifted to her lips a poison-bearing ring, a gift from the late pope, and her servants carried her away.

※

The next day, Giacinto Carrera, disgraced cardinal and Bishop of Foligno, received this letter:

> *Very Faithful Friend,*
> *The Emperor has slept in my bed. I have been the delight of a pope and I have excited cardinals with passion. I have numbered among my lovers young men astonished by their good fortune and old ones respectful of my caprices; artists who forgot to please me because my beauty intoxicated them; devotees who adored me un-ingenuously; poets who dreamed in my arms of the women they had not had; Castilians as stupid as goats, and melancholy Teutons; men of all nations, and even those who sterile love required the special spice of obscenity. I have been loved enough to be the envy of my peers and I have disarmed their jealousy.*

(Oh, very faithful friend, what a confession—if it were one!)

What remains to me?

The unexpected?

I can scarcely believe that there is anything unexpected for a woman of my beauty, my age and my liberty. All risks have confronted me and I have taken them all, even if they had nothing for seduction but Harlequin's bat or Pantaloon's coat.

Amour? Yet more amour?

I have loved too much to believe in it henceforth and I have been loved too much for tomorrow's love to have the power to make me forget yesterday's.

Remember, most faithful friend, that Cristoforo of Naples—whose genius troubled Michelangelo while he was only twenty-three years old—killed himself for me, and that I adored him, and wept for him, and forgot him, so completely that I can no longer recall the color of his eyes: the eyes of Cristoforo, once my joy, my Heaven, my Lake of Nemi, my Gulf of Naples!

No, most faithful friend, there is no hope left to me but the determination to die beautiful; that will be my final voluptuousness.

The Revolt of the Plebs

THE handsome, strong, regal male, the jovial red-haired executioner, stopped at crossroads and, a grotesque negro having blown into a marine conch that rendered powerful and sweet sounds, as if coming from on high, cried out in his fine voice of appeal:

"To the most beautiful! To the most beautiful!"

He cried, and then he whipped his mule, clad in gold-trimmed leather decorated with red smiles, and further on, among the contented people and pensive girls, he cried again: "To the most beautiful! To the most beautiful!"

When he arrived outside the queen's palace, he dismounted from his mule decorated with red smiles and shouted his cry on his knees: "To the most beautiful! To the most beautiful!"

Then a crimson cloth rose from the entrails of the tower and floated above the crenellations, while eight bronze soldiers played amorous tunes on ivory trumpets.

The queen appeared under the crimson cloth, folded into a canopy, the corners of which were held by amazons who displayed, in place of their shaven breasts, silver balls bristling with golden spikes; a skillful play lifted her up three times, like an apparition, higher than the crenellated wall, and the people, with one voice, cried in their turn, confounding in a unique adoration the elect of the purple and the future elect of the blood.

"To the most beautiful! To the most beautiful!"

At the third play the queen descended and did not rise again; the crowd fell silent, the crimson veil collapsed, the bronze heralds lowered their trumpets and the jovial red-haired executioner, bestriding his mule with red smiles, continued his route through the streets, stopping at the crossroads and crying, after the summons of the conch, in his fine voice of appeal: "To the most beautiful! To the most beautiful!"

※

The evening feasts were solemn and mild.

"You are the most beautiful," said lovers to their beauties. "Tomorrow, you'll be chosen and I won't see you again. Let me intoxicate myself forever at the twin cup of your pure breasts and penetrate you one last time, in order that a god might be born of me in other worlds!"

But the beloved sighed and said: "I'm not the most beautiful. You'll see; I'll be disdained, we'll rediscover our days and nights. Let me bathe and perfume myself, let me sleep, in order that my eyes will be calm; leave me; you can love me tomorrow. I want Him to choose me—for the next time."

Having heard that, the lovers were saddened and said: "You're the most beautiful! He'll choose you tomorrow. Give me the last pleasures, in order that an immortal god might be born from my mortal flesh."

And the beauties, softened by the certainty of their unique and sure beauty, loved heir lovers—for the last time.

"Yes," they said, vanquished, "it's only too true; I'm the most beautiful, I sense that I'm already elected."

The trumpets of the dawn woke them up, swooning with love and pride.

※

The mountain of the sacrifice rose up like a cape on the edge of green waves, bearing at its summit the statue of the god, eternally veiled in white. He was standing, pulling back over his breast with folded arms the folds of a heavy silver mantle. For, having seen him naked for a few seconds every year, the people divined and loved his imperishable beauty, his virgin and immaculate grace—for although the most beautiful was offered to him, he only wanted the simulacrum, and his arms had never knotted, like those of an impure Baal, around the quivering flesh; the one who died for him did not die under obscene and torrid kisses, but, a holocaust of amour, shedding sacred blood decently.

The crowd adored mutely, kneeling in the plain, their ecstatic eyes on the idol or, less elevated, on the queen, who, half way up beneath her crimson dais, was bemoaning, in accordance with the rite, the misfortune of not being able, having been elected the Power, to be elected the Beauty.

When the sun attained a certain point in the sky known to him alone, the jovial red-haired executioner appeared on the mountain in order to dispose at the feet of the god a block of wood wrapped in precious fabrics, but he retired immediately behind the statue, awaiting the signal of amour.

At that moment, the procession commenced. Clad in white veils, like the Lover whose conquest they desired, one by one, the young women climbed the holy mountain and, after passing slowly before the motionless god, they went down again by another path.

They passed by and came down again, sad and weeping, to come to arrange themselves around the queen, the cortege of the disdained, and that part of the mountain resounded with a terrible noise of sobbing, which, like the floods of a torrent of shame, came to fall back upon the kneeling people.

All of them had passed, and none had been chosen!

All of them? No, there was one more, but so pale and so indecisive in climbing the road that she was divined to be incredulous, perhaps a blasphemer.

"Go on, go on!" cried the crowd. "It's you! He's waiting. Go on, go on! Climb courageously. Climb, you're beautiful. Climb, you're the most beautiful!"

And at each cry of the crowd, as if borne by the power of the word, the victim took a step forward.

She arrived under the statue; the arms of the god opened momentarily, extended in a cross like two great white wings—and the people, moved, said with a divine joy: "That's the one who has been chosen! Thank you! Glory to God! Glory to God!"

Meanwhile, paler still and tottering, but resigned, the Victim, imitating the gestures of the god, extended her white arms toward the intoxicated crowd, whose members adored the beauty desired by the Mystery.

That action of a priestess, the piety of the people, the absolute consciousness of truly being "the most beautiful," the role of hierophant and holocaust, all finally affirmed the young woman, and without even glancing toward the man lost in the assembly of the faithful who was glorifying dolorously in having such a friend, she knelt down and placed her white forehead on the block clad in precious fabrics. The jovial red-haired executioner was seen to advance, and while crying in his fine voice of appeal: "The most beautiful! The most beautiful! The most beautiful!" he drew from its scabbard the naked blade of sacrifice.

Over the inclined neck the blade fell.

Then the jovial red-haired executioner took the fortunate head of the most beautiful by the hair, and with a broad gesture, he threw it into the sea.

The golden hair, a heavy fabric, allowed the fortunate head to fall slowly in the blue sky, like a divine gift; the golden hair opened in a fan of benediction and the blue sky, for a flash, was illuminated by a second sun

The people cried, in a tone of love and pity: "O most beautiful head, may your blood bless us!"

The head sank gently into the sea.

✷

"Sire," said Amalio, "The people are in revolt!"

"Why?"

"Sire, does one know why the wind that was passing softly, odorously and nonchalantly a moment ago, blows tempestuously?"

"Go and interrogate the ringleaders. Let them state their desire; I shall accomplish it, if it is just."

"Sire, they won't be able to respond to me."

"Interrogate them anyway."

"Sire, only your archers can make themselves understood."

"Shut up and go."

When his minister had gone out, Sansovino resumed his impatient march of a princely prisoner of anxiety. Strong, but alone against the delirium of crowds, he doubted a strength that had not been able to pacify hurricanes, and internally, he denied the glory of power.

Master of himself, however, and his eyes full of irony, he sought the secret, perhaps distant, cause of the disconcerting revolt, and, stopping here and there, he seemed to interrogate the old confidants of his sovereignty and its guardians, the double rank of marble heroes, the enigmatic armor and incorruptible bodies left there by insouciant souls; and he also addressed questions to the aureoled beings ecstatic in the eternal splendor of the mosaics; and he interrogated too, but with a softer gaze, his mistress Fulvia, a kind of gilded yellow reptile who was coiled up half-naked in a corner, wallowing among precious silks, eating oranges and playing with a monkey.

The animal continually entangled itself in the fabrics or in Fulvia's dress, a short tunic of red cotton embroidered with the black heads of baboons; then it became annoyed, showed its teeth, but immediately calmed down, making a velvet paw, caressing the neck, shoulders and breasts of her friend, in imitation of Sansovino, and then laughed and inflated its cheeks.

"Fulvia," said the prince, "I forbid you to allow yourself to be caressed by Angiolo. He'll bite you, and you know that I don't like blood."

"Blood, blood!" cried Fulvia. "Blood is beautiful. It's the crimson liquid, the living liquid!"

A gesture made her fall silent, and she retreated into the corner. "Be good, Angiolo! The lord has said that you must be good. Here, look, your portrait, there, and there again, look, look, look . . ."

And, ingenuous or perverse, she lifted up the flap of her short robe, laying bare her frail and pure loins, the amiable profile of her belly, virgin of fruit.

Suddenly—fear causes modesty—she stopped playing, lowered her dress and tucked it between her legs like a wrestler. Angiolo also froze, like a grotesque statuette of dread, and, his hand clutching Fulvia's, he trembled.

Sansovino stopped dead, his hand on his dagger.

A composite voice rose up, the barking of an infernal pack, as strident as rigging slapping the masts in a tempest and sails flapping in despair: "The Beheadings! The Beheadings! The Beheadings!"

Amalio came back.

"Well?"

"It's the Beheadings, sire."

"Haven't I suppressed them?" said Sansovino. "Haven't I annihilated that cruel festival in which a dozen heads of virgins fall without glory and without expiations solely for the safeguard of a criminal and foolish tradition? In ancient times, you know, there was only one. Two were soon required, then four, then twelve, for the stupid superstition of the plebs and priests. Twelve crimes to honor the infinite! Amalio, I came and I've protected my people against themselves; I forbade all bloody sacrifices; no dozen heads, nor even one. No more blood! What are they demanding, then? Am I not obeyed?"

"You are obeyed, Sire. So I don't understand."

"Then what good are you? Go back, bring me one of these savages, a leader, if they have any. Yes, the Plebs always have leaders. The leaders are the conscience of the crowd. Bring me the conscience of the crowd, that I might sound it, that I might sink my arm into the secret of those tenebrous entrails."

"I know what they want, Prince," said Fulvia.

"Shut up and get dressed. The People are going to come in, and they don't like beauty. Beauty surprises them and makes them angry."

Fulvia obeyed.

"Come on, Angiolo, and be good, very good. Come on, friend, and I'll tell you a story. Shh! You don't know what the festival of the Beheaders is? Listen carefully! Oh, it's so fine! Can you imagine that every year, at Easter, when the sun rises and blossoms like a great flower of amour... have you ever been in love, Angiolo?

". . . twelve beautiful girls three times six years old, and blonde like Him, were sacrificed for the City and died in order to perpetuate life . . .

"They went, dressed in white like brides, to the mountain of the East, and there they were stripped of all their adornments and, naked, kissed one another on the mouth and then knelt down, and the red man cut off their heads. He was beautiful too, the red man, and tall and strong. Twelve times the ax fell, and his arms didn't weaken. Of, the beautiful fête! The entire Populace was there, weeping amorously, singing hymns to the God, so good, who gives life with joy and to whom it's necessary to render it with joy.

"Blood, blood, my little Angiolo! The beautiful pure blood flowed over the sides of the mountain of marble, and the virgins drank a drop of beautiful pure and virginal blood, in order to become apt for amour and childbirth. Now, the girls are neglected and they'll be sterile. Oh, Sansovino, why have you forbidden the fête? Are you asleep, my little Angiolo:

Go to bye-byes. Angiolo,
Go to by-byes, little Angiolo!

"What do you want?" Sansovino asked the leader of the People whom Amalio pushed toward the prince.

"The Beheadings, Sire."

"They're abolished."

"Reestablish them, Sire, if you love us. The twelve are ready, they're here, with us. Do you want to see them? Come, Lucia, Corona, Palma, all of you!"

The twelve virgins came in, pale, with ardent eyes. They were holding hands. They bowed to the prince and Lucia, in a severe and slightly tremulous voice, said, slowly: "We beg you, Prince, to permit the Beheadings."

Sansovino made no reply.

Then another chief came in, almost naked, his breast hairy and red. He lifted his staff and said: "I am the People. The People want the Beheadings."

Sansovino replied to the People: "I no longer have an executioner. Who will be the red man?"

"Me," said the People.

"Go," said Sansovino, "and let the people be their own executioner."

The men left, the twelve virgins left, and a violent cry of joy, a voluptuous howl, entered through the narrow windows. The delirious people were singing, indefatigably, in a drunken fashion:

"To the Beheadings! To the Beheadings! To the Beheadings! Glory to God! Glory to Sansovino!"

Fulvia, bounding from her corner, with Angiolo in her arms, ran to the prince.

"You're good! You're good, Sansovino! How I love you!"

But the prince, thrusting her aside, inclined his head over the shoulder of the sad Amalio, and he wept.

The Royal Accident

THE young king and the young queen made their entrance through the royal gate; it was a breach that was opened in the wall on solemn occasions, when the king came back, dead or alive, from a war and a victory. Ancestors of the young king had crossed the breach a dozen times, which had been made a dozen times over and repaired a dozen times; but for a long time, for generations, the royal gate had remained walled up, and ivy had established its idleness there, a symbol of peace and decadence.

The ivy was torn away and the victor entered.

The cortege was simple and magnificent: first, squadrons of cavaliers, manes in the wind and lances in their fists; then, in an uncovered carriage, the king and the queen, the king, tightly-wrapped like a bee in a corselet of auroral velvet, embroidered with hyacinths, and the queen, like a dragonfly, in a corselet of violet silk embroidered with topazes; all round the carriages was a cavalcade of guards; and finally, closing the march, foot-soldiers with iron helmets, their shoulders pliant beneath long and heavy arquebuses.

Respectful and curious, the crowd pressed, without cordiality and without joy; its members seemed sullen, thinking that they had been frustrated of the celebrations of the royal wedding, and that the victor was bringing them, in the daughter of the vanquished king, not so much a queen as a crowned slave.

However, the young queen smiled, and the king saluted his people.

Moments passed thus and the cortege advanced slowly, but without jolts, without tempests; the gilded carriage resembled a majestic galley on calm waters.

Too much mildness on the part of the people makes kings anxious, as an excessively calm sea worries captains. The young queen, the daughter of the vanquished, leaned toward her husband and, while continuing to smile at the people, pronounced a few words doubtless agreed in advance, for the king was unmoved and only responded with a sign. An aide-de-camp having turned his eyes toward the royal vehicle, the young king raised his hand ingenuously to his chin; the aide-de-camp repeated the gesture, but no immediate incident was the consequence of that mysterious exchange of brief thoughts.

Gradually, the crowd grew, and a visible swell agitated the surface of the tranquil ocean slightly; there were currents and eddies, but they were peaceful, gentle and silent. Finally, they turned into a broader street, not completely cleared, for the cortege had progressed with a relative and unexpected rapidity; the lingerers flocked toward the houses, intimidated by the horses, the lances and the brutal aspect of the cavaliers. The train slowed down, but suddenly without any apparent cause, one of the horses of the carriage veered sideways; the rig, manned by subtle postillions, hesitated momentarily, and was then thrown violently to the left. The line of guards was broken, imprudent individuals advanced; one of them fell under the feet of the horses.

Then, abruptly, like a circus rig, the royal carriage resumed its position, the six horses calmed down, now motionless.

The king leapt down and was the first to reach the wounded man, whom he lifted in his arms. Instantly, from the crowd, previously so calm and almost mute, a rumble rose that soon burst, like a formidable thunderclap of acclamation. To the inactive people looking on, the king's action seemed a marvel of propriety and heroism: the horses suddenly stopping, the king leaping down from his carriage, racing to aid a stranger, doubtless a victim of his imprudence and curiosity—what an occasion for enthusiasm!

But when the crowd saw the young king install the wounded man personally on the royal cushions, beside the queen, who hastened to wipe his face and hands, there was an indescribable delirium—and even the army, forgetting its role, intoned frenetic hurrahs.

"What a good king!" said the people. "What a good queen! There's only one king to be so good! There's only one queen to be so good! And how handsome they are! The king has a truly royal nose, and the queen has eyes as soft as the eyes of the Madonna!"

The crowd softened; a fuse of amorous cries caught fire along the streets, to the walls and beyond, as far as the fields and the forests, all the way to the mountains.

Meanwhile, the surgeons had come running and a carriage had been summoned to transport the wounded man.

"Take him to my palace," said the king. "He'll be cared for like my brother."

Those words, soon repeated by all mouths into all ears, further augmented a delirium that was reaching paroxysm; they crossed doors, windows and partitions, rose to the attics and descended to the cellars; and the whole city spread out into the streets. The blind wept because they could not see; the deaf wept because they could not hear; the paralyzed and the feverish dragged themselves to the window-sills.

The human mass became so compact that it took an hour to cross half of the main square. From time to time, the king stood up, waving his cap with swan's plumes, and vortices of cries sprang up, falling back in cataracts. He took the young queen, made her climb up on the cushions, and showed her to the people; then the joy and admiration were so great that means of expression would fail. There was a minute of religious silence, as at the elevation of the holy sacrament.

Suddenly, as if vanquished, the queen let her head fall upon her husband's shoulder; the king kissed the forehead that approached his lips—and the spectacle of that royal idyll suddenly reignited the enthusiasm that had quieted; the popular volcano launched forth a sheaf of flames.

Meanwhile, a movement was organized in the crowd, which opened up to let strong and resolute men pass. When there were about thirty around the royal carriage their determination became clearly visible; they unhitched the horses, took their place, and with great joy, began hailing their masters.

It is thus that such ovations ordinarily finish; humans cannot imagine a more manifest sign of servitude.

The delirium increased; women risked being crushed to come and kiss the dust of the royal footstep.

In the midst of the heroic clamors, the cortege set off again, while the young queen squeezed the hand of the young king convulsively.

They looked at one another; there was amour in their eyes.

The Queen's Hands

AFTER the midday meal, a spectacle given to the court, a rigorous ceremonial in which it was necessary to offer sovereign gestures and inimitable graces to the admiration of the courtiers, the king and the queen reposed in an intimate solitude. Their favorite corner was a little pavilion that stood on the grand canal; it was a marvelously melancholy place; nothing could be heard there but the monotonous plaint of sad poplars, and sometimes the noise of a battle of white wings against black wings—swans proclaiming in vain the mystery unexpressed by the visible peace.

On entering the reserved chamber, to which long corridors had led them, the king and queen found another table laid, with a meal no longer pompous, a simple snack that had nothing royal except the whimsy of the dishes, the rarity of the fruits and the fabulous antiquity of the wines: the tongues of pink flamingoes smoked over juniper wood, Asian peaches no larger than walnuts, Galilean wine from vines blessed by Jesus. But for some time there had been less pleasure in dining in secret, and often, without even looking at the little table, the queen began braiding threads of silk, silently.

For weeks, already, the queen had been manipulating the silk threads and the singular work had been occupying the pleasure of her fingers. She took three threads, assorted or contrasted in accordance with their colors, and, twisting them together, she fashioned a triple thread, still very fine and extremely sturdy.

"What are you doing, my queen?"

"Tripling silk threads," the queen replied.

"I can see that," said the king. "Your slender fingers are going back and forth, you're moistening your thumb with the tip of your tongue and you're twisting and twisting the lovely silk threads—but why?"

"To amuse myself," the queen replied.

"And when you've twisted all your silks?"

"I won't twist all my silks," replied the queen. "I'll only twist the prettiest, the most delicate and the most supple. That's why my work is taking so long; but have no fear, my dear king, I won't wear away my fingers. My work is taking a long time, but it will finish, and when it finishes, there'll be a great surprise."

"For whom?" asked the king.

The queen smiled, without responding, and her hands sometimes trembled a little and tangled the threads, so soft were the king's eyes and so anxious was his voice.

Having obtained no other response, the king asked no more questions, and, sitting at the queen's feet like a good page, he drew long sobs from a dolorous viol.

He was such a melancholy king!

Nothing had ever been able to satisfy him. Every joy was only half-sweet, and, anxiously, he wept for the half of the joy that escaped him. That was the best, the purest, the sweetest, and it fled, it went away toward infinity, an odorous smoke that laughed at desire. All pain was proportionately bitter to him, for he felt pain twice over, and the most fugitive, touched by amour for a heart so tender, settled familiarly on his forehead and surrounded it with an aureole of luminous dolor.

He approached his lips to the queen's hands and gently, without hindering their mysterious labor, he kissed them one after the other, several times. Then he raised his head and said: "Queen, why do you love me less?"

"King, why are you asking me that?"

"I'm asking you in order to be consoled by the love in your voice."

The queen replied: "Well, be consoled. Your question is foolish; that is my reply."

"Queen, my question isn't foolish, since you don't know how to reply to it. If my question were foolish, you would have closed my lips with a big irresistible kiss—and you haven't done it. You haven't budged, you haven't blushed, and your fingers haven't suspended their alarming work . . ."

"Alarming?"

"Yes, alarming. The perpetual movement of those fingers frightens me."

"Oh, fear!"

"Yes, fear! As a child is frightened by seeing things move that ought not to be moving."

"But fingers are made to move!" said the queen.
"Not like that! Not like that!"

The king got up. Drawing away a few paces, he remained standing, fascinated by the movement of the queen's white hands. By virtue of following their sinuous but regular movement he succeeded in foreseeing all the little gestures of the fingers; the nail of the ring-finger was about to pass there and glint; the ring on the index-finger was about to appear in profile, and in the following gesture, it was going to shine with all the ocular splendor of its sapphire . . .

There was an unforeseen gesture, and then everything stopped.

Now the queen was playing with the work of her hands; a long serpent of silk seemed truly to be uncoiling in living spirals.

The king was still standing, immobile and staring. He did not see the movements that the queen was making; he could still see those that she was not making. She stood up, her eyes more luminous than the scales of the silken serpent that was writhing under her fingers, and it seemed that, having fashioned the simulacrum, she had acquired, by virtue of her work, a new and sudden soul, the hissing and venomous soul of a viper.

The fascination of the eyes had replaced the fascination of the fingers; under the queen's gaze, the king advanced. She touched his shoulder; he stopped. At that moment, the serpent hissed and bit—and the strangled king fell to his knees, and then lay down on his side.

The queen opened the window and made a sign.

The swans were battling on the green water of the grand canal, where the sad poplars were weeping all their leaves.

The black wings were battling the white wings; the white wings were vanquished and they floated over the slow waters of the grand canal, like crimes that would never be buried.

The Cowshed
A Christmas Story

WHEN Prince Astere was twenty years old, he decided to marry, and imparted that royal desire—which is to say, that royal determination—to his ministers. Respectfully, they were astonished, and reminded him that he had been betrothed, since the age of twelve, to a princess then in swaddling clothes, but who already promised to be more beautiful than the day, for whom the fays had predicted a fortune worthy of Semiramis. But Prince Astere replied that he was twenty and the princess precisely eight years old, and that he was not in a mood to wait for the flowering of that incomparable little girl in order to love.

Then the ministers protested, while bowing: "Prince, all the beauties in your realm would climb into your bed at a sign of your pleasure, and our wives, even our daughters . . ."

"I'm weary of your daughters and your wives," said the prince. "I'm weary of the servants of my realm; I want a wife whom I can make my wife, and I shall only know her; she will smile when I open her bedroom door, like a friend, and not like a slave. She will be a great economy for the State," Prince Astere continued, in a severe tone, "for you have cost me dear, gentlemen, and the skin of your progeniture is not worth either the brocade in which I have dressed them or the ducats with which I have weighed down your pockets. And as for your wives, come on, I'm no longer fifteen years old."

The ministers looked at one another, and, fearing to lose their places and their decorations, they kept silent.

"This is what I have decided," said Prince Astere. "An edict will be issued, which will summon to my palace all the young women of my age, rich or poor, noble or common, and as they arrive, they will be taken everywhere; they will be shown all the marvels of my treasures, they will be served the most exquisite meals, they will be enabled to hear the sweetest music, and when evening comes, they will be allowed to choose, in order to spend the night, between the cowshed and the palace, between the royal bed and the bale of straw on which the baby Jesus slept."

"There will be very few in the stable," said the prime minister.

"That's probable," said Prince Astere.

※

The edict was issued, and the virgin pilgrims headed toward the prince's abode. Some arrived accompanied by their families, their friends, their servants, and all those who, confident in the beauty of the candidate, hoped by their servility to entitle themselves to future favors. Others arrived alone, either strong in their purity and sufficiently protected by such armor, or lustful, even courtesans, thinking to capture the prince by their boldness or their science, all ready to climb from male to male all the way to the throne.

Both kinds arrived, and were treated as possible queens; they were all received similarly, with the most scrupulous regard; however, the richest or the most beautiful, and particularly those who had the double gift of wealth and beauty, found a more urgent and more deferential welcome; they were offered the most odorous flowers and the most perfumed jam, and the most comfortable and best furnished chambers of the palace were indicated to them by the chamberlains

As Prince Astere's ministers had foreseen, none of the beauties had chosen the cows and the bed of straw; at the offer of a night among the worthy cows and the gentle heifers, they all started to laugh, believing it to be an agreeable joke, and thinking: *God, what a witty court!*

※

Every evening, however, shortly before midnight, Prince Astere, dressed like an oxherd, but an oxherd of noble elegance, went to the cowshed alone. In one hand he held a long oak staff, and in the other, a poor hooded lantern with horn windows; shod in smoked clogs, he went out by a secret door, making as little noise as possible, and set forth firmly along the dark paths that led to the farm, some distance from his palace. The young candidates were taken there in carriages; he, the prince, went on foot, like a laborer returning to his poor bed of straw; and while walking through the mud, he fantasized.

He wondered whether he might find, huddled under the fresh straw, the angel with the humble heart and the pure eyes that Heaven ought to send him, the adorable young woman who had understood that poverty is the road to exaltation and that, to arrive at the king's bed, it was necessary to pass through the door of the cowshed.

But he always found the cowshed empty, and although he sounded the straw with his long oak staff and illuminated every corner of the worthy heifers' abode with his lantern, he did not see anything, and found nothing but the worthy heifers, asleep, with wisps of straw dangling from their dewlaps. He caressed them, stayed there for a while inhaling the warm and musky air, and then left and, having dropped the wooden latch, sadly resumed his path, returned to the palace and went to bed, afflicted by the pride of virgins.

※

Now, it happened that a shepherdess, who grazed her sheep far away from there, and far from any city, heard mention of the edict. She was twenty years old and thought that she was pretty, but although her heart was pure, her body was soiled. The local shepherds made use of her in a familiar fashion, and she was so benevolent that she did not refuse any of them, no matter how poor or ugly; thus, her reputation was very bad and the women encouraged little children coming home from school to throw stones at her and call her "slut."

> *They call me a slut,*
> *With my clogs, hi ho,*
> *They call me a slut.*

Nevertheless, she set forth. As the edict assured all those who were going to the palace food, and even a mule to make the journey, she told herself that it was a fine opportunity to see new things, and who could tell? If she did not captivate the prince—which she scarcely imagined—perhaps she would please some lord who would give her a gold coin to put in her bosom. So she set forth.

Her friends the shepherds had told her that she would see marvelous things, such as only exist on the Moon or in the Empire of the Antipodes, but everything she imagined was surpassed by what she saw, because her imagination was as poor as her shepherdess's smock. She thought the sweetness of perfumes and musk would make her ill, and she was given jam to eat so delicate that she thought she might never enjoy the taste of burnets or wild strawberries again.

The chamberlains showed her the room that was destined for her; it was the least beautiful in the entire palace, but its luxury was still rather seductive, for the walls were hung with tapestries in which unicorns played, and on the floor, formed by elaborate mosaics, the fleeces of blue goats were accumulated, softer than pillows of moss and carpets of dry leaves. The bed was gilded wood, the curtains were multicolored silk, and it was as broad, high and profound as the shadow and silence of an autumnal forest.

She was already rejoicing in sleeping by night in such rich surroundings when the chamberlains added, in a tone of incomprehensible irony: "Now we're going to show you a room even more beautiful—perhaps!—and you can choose."

A carriage was waiting, into which she climbed, and they were soon at the farm.

"This," said the chamberlains, "is a cowshed."

The shepherdess went into the cowshed, and the heifers, which were ruminating, turned their heads toward her, as if to salute her; she caressed them too; she gave them names, and the worthy beasts stretched out their muzzles and opened their soft eyes wide.

"Well, I'll stay here," said the shepherdess, after making a tour of the cowshed. "The other room is beautiful, but in truth, this one is even more beautiful—and how well I shall sleep on this bed of straw! Close the door as you leave; I feel at home. Good night!"

※

Prince Astere was in despair. Thirty times he had put on his smoked clogs, picked up his oak staff and lit his horn lantern; thirty times he had made the pilgrimage to the cowshed in vain.

Let's go, he said to himself, the thirty-first time. *I'll go once more, and if I don't find anyone there, I'll issue a new edict to annul the first, and I'll be very annoyed. O Lord, enable me to find the elect!*

He lifted the latch, and without going in, he darted an almost-distracted glance into the stable; he no longer had faith.

He was about to leave without searching any further, slightly ashamed of his candor, when the straw stirred, just under the manger, near the sleeping muzzle of an old brown cow whose milk had sated his thirst many a time.

The shepherdess stood up, her blonde hair full of blonde straw; she was so fresh and so gracious, so childlike, with her eyes troubled by the light, that the prince knelt down, saying: "You are queen!"

"Prince," said the shepherdess, divining that her sovereign was before her, "oh, prince, I haven't come in order to be queen, I'm nothing but a poor girl and a wretched sinner. I can't abuse you; I'm . . . I'm . . . a fallen woman!"

She wept and moaned so much that her poor worn bodice split under the effort of the sobs, revealing two little candid and fearful breasts, while the prince, kissing her hand, simply repeated:

"You are queen, you are queen, you are queen!"

The City of the Sphinxes

THERE was a marvelous city that rose up in the middle of a great desert, so vast that it enclosed in its walls meadows full of livestock, fields of crops, forests, orchards, springs and an amorous lake where the young women went to bathe in the nude on the third day of the new moon.

No one had ever entered the marvelous city, and no one had ever left it.

It extended in the middle of the great desert, proud of being unique, in being the world, in being life, in being the joy fallen from the heavens amid the infinite sadness of the sands.

Its inhabitants, mild, simple and voluptuous, were ignorant of the forms of a precise religion and the tyranny of a strict government, like the divine Indians whom Benjamin of Tudela visited, who knew no other magistracy than good will.[1] However, the sight of the

---

1 Rabbi Benjamin of Tudela (1130-1173) travelled extensively in Europe, north Africa and western Asia and published graphic descriptions of what he found there; although he did not get as far as India he did gather information in the near East as to what might be found there and in China.

marvels that burst forth on their horizon had enabled them to conceive the possibility of future delights, the probable prolongation beyond death of the enjoyments of their humanity.

For a long distance around the walls there was nothing but sand, stones or little white rocks like old bones, but out there, near the circle, on very clear days, it was possible to distinguish miraculous forests, all shades of blue, a high white tower capped with gold, and, toward the sunset, a roseate palace with a thousand windows of light; flocks of angels flew above the treetops, and their wings inscribed flashes of lightning in the pure air.

Those marvels consoled the inhabitants of the unique city at the hour of their death. They imagined a migration of souls toward the blue forests, toward the white tower capped with gold and the palace with a thousand windows of light; they saw themselves, angelic and immortally joyful, their wings striping the pure air with lightning flashes; and the voluptuousness of soaring above the treetops seemed so sweet to them that some died voluntarily, because of the desire for such a metamorphosis.

Fortunate as the people were, the idea of a happiness that drowns in darkness was insupportable to them; they aspired to absolute pleasure, and did not want to comprehend the rights of death, the infelicity of life that induces humans to desire to dissolve like a grain of salt in the ocean of oblivion; so they believed in the perpetuity of their innocent souls, not by virtue of dogma or doctrine, but as one believes in the veracity of a charming tale and the caresses of an illusion.

No one in that land cared any longer about the truth; they admitted the axiom: *The truth is what I believe.* And they permitted others to have their own truth, as one has a pet dog or caged birds. There was a legend regarding the Truth, which represented it as a kind of bogey-man, who stupefied children and the impudent with a single glance; some people, doubtless by divination, depicted it as a hateful and ferocious monster that grabbed human beings by one leg and made use of them as clubs to crush other humans.

(Those simple folk, on the day when they wanted gods, would doubtless have adopted as a patron candid Liberty, a woman with large indulgent eyes, a creature of love and grace, with a proud gesture.)

No one in that land, therefore, had ever had the idea of going to see whether the distant marvels of the horizon were true marvels, edifications worthy of faith, authentic trees and real angels; no one had ever attempted to cross the threshold watched by the two sphinxes.

Beasts of bronze, but oracular, alive when it pleased them to be, frightful works of a preadamite magic, two sphinxes guarded the city's only gate, the gate through which it was forbidden to go out. They smiled in their brazen sleep, the two guardian beasts established there by Istakar, the founder of the city; and, as mediators, they seemed only to have chosen the immobility of death out of disdain for the action of life. Sometimes, words emerged from their immutable lips: there were poems or tales so ancient that they were scarcely comprehensible any longer; but, collected and written down, they served as talismans and formulae of amour. Sphinx and sphinge,[1] at the moment of nobility, adolescents came to visit the beasts of bronze and kiss them on the mouth; the young women kissed the mouth of the beast whose face was triangulated by a pointed beard, and males kissed the mouth of the beast that had female breasts.

One day, an adolescent, already as strong as a man and more learned than an old man, after having kissed the mouth of the sphinge, touched with his lips the nipples of the bronze breasts and said: "Sphinge, reply to me."

The sphinge responded: "Child, how have you found the secret of Istakar?"

"I've found it, since you're replying to me."

"Come back tomorrow," said the sphinge. "It's the day when the people amuse themselves at the game of the sacred bath, the day when, for the first time, the young women blossomed during the year to the amorous life show themselves naked on the shores of the lake. Instead of following the people, come here, and I'll do as you wish, since you know the secret of Istakar."

The next day, as soon as the adolescent had arrived, a little door opened slowly in the wall, while the sphinge, in a lamentable voice, pronounced the single word: "Go."

---

1 A *sphinge*, or *sphynge* is a female sphinx; English does not differentiate the sexes of the species, but French does, and as it is important to do so in the context of the present story I have followed the French practice.

Then the adolescent entered into the exterior world. He walked for a long time, his eyes raised toward the distant blue forests, the white towers capped with gold, the windows of light, and the radiant flight of angels—so long that night fell upon the desert, and he went to sleep.

Three times night fell upon the desert, and three times the adolescent went to sleep with his head on a stone.

On the fourth day, in the morning, as he extended his imploring and weary arms toward the marvels of the horizon, still as distant and still as beautiful, an eagle swooped down and alighted on the stone where he was asleep.

"Eagle," said the adolescent, "have pity on me; pick me up and carry me out there, to the summit of the ivory tower."

The eagle took hold of the adolescent.

"Adolescent, lie down on my back, between my two wings, and I'll carry you to the ivory tower."

The eagle flew away, like Geryon,[1] and the adolescent lay down between its two wings, exalted by amour, his gaze stubbornly fixed on the white tower capped with gold, still distant and still beautiful.

The eagle flew for a long time, so long that they arrived in the land where the days are years and the years are centuries, and still the tower stood on the horizon,

---

[1] The reference is not to the Geryon of Greek myth but to the Geryon of Dante's *Inferno*, the winged monster that carries Dante and Virgil on its back to the circle of Fraud.

amid the flight of angels, above the blue forest and the palace with windows of light.

Every century, the adolescent asked with the anxiety of desire: "Eagle, will we arrive soon?"

But the eagle, without replying, flapped its wings violently, and they passed over the land where the flowers are suns and the women attach stars to their ears, and still the ivory tower was resplendent in the distance, still pure and still beautiful.

"Eagle, will we arrive soon?" asked the adolescent, in a sad and hoarse voice. "Eagle, my hands have become yellow and my hair has turned entirely white. Eagle, will we arrive soon?"

"We have arrived, old man," replied the eagle, alighting on the stone on which the adolescent had laid his head on the third night of his journey. "Here is the tower, here is the forest, here is the palace, here are the angels, such as you saw them when I took you between my two wings; we have gone around the world without attaining your desire, and now you're old, you're going to die, but at least you're going to die at home."

The eagle disappeared, having shaken off its burden; and, having fallen rudely on the stones, the old man went to sleep and dreamed.

The first thing he did when he awoke was to search with his fatigued eyes for the divine marvels for which he had nourished amour for so long, but the horizon was bare, only forming a black circle. He was not surprised, for his dream had prepared him finally to know and comprehend the truth; saddened by a lost light, he rejoiced in knowing that the horizon was a black circle, and, scorning the primitive illusions of humans, marching without repose, he only took two days to reach the gate guarded by the sphinxes.

It was open.

He went in and said: "O sphinx, friend of my youth, here I am. I've come back from such a long voyage that my hands are all yellow and my hair is completely white—but I know the truth. There is no blue forest out there, nor a white tower capped with gold, nor a palace with windows of light, not a radiant flock of archangels; I have traveled the world and the worlds, lying on an eagle's back, and now I know; I know that the world is ringed by a black circle made of darkness, and that the marvel of the horizons is only the futile flower of eternal Illusion. I know, and I shall kill Illusion. I know, and I shall tell the truth. People, this is the truth . . ."

But the sphinge, at the sign made to her by the bronze male, stood up sadly, and crushed beneath her claw, like a compassionate lioness, the monster who had traversed the worlds between Geryon's wings.

Part Two:

Women's faces

Irmine

WITH her pretty name, almost unprecedented, her hair the color of the flax of distaffs, her white face, her long and supple body, and her elegant hands, Irmine seemed a kind of masterpiece of a young woman, an example for her future sisters, the model of what that kind of chrysalis can produce of the delectable and the delicate. And she had talents: coloring previously-traced trees, in accordance with the Cassagne method,[1] or windmills whose wheels churned the water of the little river that came from far away, or the cottage whose chimneys smoked placidly, as indicated by the blue-tinted spirals; and then, the effects of snow, the effects of moonlight, the effects of storms, and in general anything that nature, seen by the eye of a drawing teacher, can offer of melancholy and picturesque rococo.

---

1 Armand Cassagne (1823-1907) was the author of the oft-reprinted *L'Alphabet du dessin* (1880), aimed at children, which proposed a systematic geometrical method of drawing. An 1884 sequel *Guide des modèles à silhouette* recommended tracing silhouettes as a first step in constructing pictures, including landscapes.

Irmine was therefore celebrated in the small town where she walked on feast days in esthetic costumes, the foremost ornament of which was a brooch in the form of a watercolor palette, on which, against a gold background, silver cups gripped fake precious stones, and a few real ones.

So pretty and so ridiculous, Irmine might have occasioned pity, but for her eyes. They were almost terrible, entirely black, fixed, imperious, disdainful and cruel. Irmine's eyes contradicted the effects of snow, the effects of moonlight, the windmills and the cottages, the palette and the silver cups; when one looked at them, and above all when they looked at you, one was sure of seeing another Irmine, and of being seen by an unknown and mysterious Irmine: the mantle of the ridiculous fell from her shoulders and one had the sensation, doubtless because of the disquieting blackness of her eyes, of a foolish but coldly passionate virgin, solely clad in the obscure transparency that the night weaves in the depths of gardens around a marble nymph.

In her entourage, Irmine's eyes were uncomprehended; they were deplored; it was her sole fault, the damage of that privileged creature. People would have liked them to be misty gray, a chaste hue, with soft blue flashes to simulate the awakening of nature on April mornings, when the fumes of evaporating white frost only allow little corners to be seen of the azure of the heavens. Other people, with calmer imaginations, regretted that they were not a unified and entirely pure blue. In sum, Irmine's eyes were an inexhaustible subject of conversation and all tastes, while manifesting their diversity, were in accord on one point: "It's a great pity that such a pretty young woman has such eyes, eyes such as have never been seen!"

However, there are lovers of eyes. One of them passed through the town of which Irmine was the glory, and, having seen Irmine's eyes, did not go any further.

That connoisseur was named Savin. He traveled eternally, all over the world, mingling with the crowds, seeking foreign gazes and new eyes. When he arrived in a city, he went to the places where people strolled, saluting one another, smiling and grimacing; it was there that he collected the most beautiful gazes, those whose spectrum extended from pity to desire. He knew how to read that complex script of glimmers and gleams like the nocturnal signals that ships exchange; he divined satisfied adulteresses and those whose hearts were eroding in an unbreachable solitude; he understood the streaks of pale light that signified indolent desires, and the rapid radiance that revealed determinations sure of being realized at the chosen time; he compared the declining flames of regret with the sharp flames of hope and the obscure phosphorescence of resignation. In deciphering them, however, he enjoyed the color most of all, and what he called, by virtue of a singular innovation, the *timbre* of gazes.

Savin distinguished the color of the eyes from the color of the gaze; according to him, yellow eyes, for instance, could give blue, green, black, red gazes: gazes of all possible colors, shades that have no name, so fugitive and so diverse that one does not encounter them twice, either in other eyes or the same eyes. In addition to those hues, however, and primarily, he observed a fundamental hue, always constant, although different from the apparent color of the eye; thus, blue eyes have for their fundamental hue a yellow-gray gaze, and dark eyes golden-yellow; that is what he called the timbre. The timbre gave the gaze its personality; he differentiated them and confirmed them in a unique and absolute hue. There are eyes almost identical in appearance, but the gazes of those eyes, by virtue of the diversity given to them by the timbre, are always dissimilar.

Having seen Irmine, Savin judged: *Her eyes are black, the timbre is golden yellow dotted with red; the hues of the gaze can rise as far as brilliance and descend as far as velvet black; I've just perceived a blue-black gaze striped with gold and a dark green gaze striped with crimson.*

And Savin continued to count all the possible gazes of Irmine's eyes, without worrying about the law of contrasting colors, for, according to him, the color of eyes and gazes was sufficiently different, in essence, from ordinary colors not to be subject to the same laws. In any case, without being scornful of science, he considered it to be a servant, only good for crude work, for sweeping the paths where people walk for pleasure; he wanted to amuse himself and be happy by means of the possession of divine eyes, with marvelous gazes such as had never been seen.

He therefore went no further, and he married Irmine, who allowed him to do so when she knew that Savin was a "good catch" and that she would be able to ornament her white neck with a palette of cups enriched with diamonds.

Then, all day long, Savin rejoiced in the play of eyes: eyes of black velvet whose somber radiance was punctuated by gold or crimson; and he searched for what Irmine's eyes were saying, in all verity.

A coldly passionate woman, solely clad in the obscure transparency of night, woven in the depths of a garden around a marble goddess.

They said that, Irmine's eyes, but they lied, as a woman's eyes do, for Irmine, having been a mediocre pupil of Cassagne, was a sage wife and a prudent mother. In her leisure hours she colored, as before, tracings in which all the rococo melancholy of an honest and sentimental nature sang: effects of moonlights, effects of snow; cottages from which a ribbon of blue rose, mills that made water foam like soapy water.

In Irmine's eyes, there was nothing but the illusion of what came to be mirrored therein; they were a beautiful stained-glass window, which, when opened, allowed the sight of a farmyard.

There was only illusion, only a lie, in Irmine's eyes. Savin adored her until death, an adorer of his own dreams, happy when visions of gold or crimson passed, like the benediction of a divine promise, through the black velvet gaze.

Phenice

SHE was a young woman like all the others. Nothing differentiated her from her sisters; everything about her seemed mediocre; her dubious blonde beauty was ordinary and insipid, her elegance barely sufficient, her intelligence, which was supposed to be non-existent, did not ignite any flame in her soft, bleak blue eyes; in truth she was very well summarized by the disdain of that brief and simple definition: a young woman like all the others.

However, after having judged her thus, all the men accorded her a *je ne sais quoi*, and they all desired her. If she had had caprices, even mad ones, or whims, even monstrous ones, attentive slaves would have devoted themselves to her pleasure, but she did not encourage either enterprises or sacrifices; she did not appear to comprehend allusions, and if anyone risked a less indirect declaration before responding with some banality, she had the amorous remark repeated two or three times—which chilled the most inflamed.

They were only put off momentarily, and Phenice loomed up again in their imagination, a lighthouse with which blinded flocks of migratory geese came to collide.

But the *je ne sais quoi* remained, an ever-obscure enigma, for it had not been given to any of her adorers to be able to reveal the secret, plucked from Phenice's mouth. Her virtue was celebrated; she had even retained after turning thirty a kind of virginal air, the astonished attitude of a perpetually surprised Diana; her husband seemed to her to be as indifferent to her as the rest of the world; she had no children.

Phenice's life was a slumber in which no one suspected dreams, a crossing of which no one divined the pleasures. However, that dormant creature dreamed; that distracted passenger saw. One day, finally, she got up from her slumber and stopped the voyage of her silent boat on a chosen sandbank.

Among the suitors of those closed lips, a young man had interested her by virtue of his melancholy discretion; she found the opportunity to let him talk and confess, in a tone of passionate sadness, his desire and his determination.

Phenice listened, this time with an appearance of comprehension, and deigned to feign a delicate emotion. Having allowed her hand to be taken, after an appropriate resistance, she said:

"People think me stupid because an amorous discourse does not excite my nerves with any esthetic frisson, and cold because I am not intoxicated by the perfume of hopeful sensualities. I'm not stupid, but it's true that no one has yet troubled the lake of indifference that is my poor heart. All your thrown stones have only made puerile ricochets over the placid waters, and the pebbles have gone to die in the distance and plunge silently into the sand, among the inattentive reeds. Uproot a rock and it falls. I would be delectably fearful, and I would raise my head to see, at least, whence a thrust of such audacity and such arms has departed. But you are only good for ricochets, children amused by teasing the monster but incapable of making it roll over. I'm waiting, full of good will, ready to respond to the appeal when the cry stirs me, when the stone has touched me; but don't touch me, for you'll have caught me, and you'll be disappointed. Perhaps you're right to play, and to slacken the grip of your arms deliberately—and be satisfied to be incapable of conquering me, for I'm not worth the trouble. In any case, I'm not unaware of the opinion you have of me: a woman like all the others, isn't it? Nothing is more true, my friend; you'll know that when you want."

The reply was given to Phenice: "I don't disdain you, since I love you. Don't confuse me with the others. I'm gathering my strength, I'll uproot a block of stone, I'll launch it over you, I'll crush you . . ."

"Crush me!" said Phenice.

"Be mine!"

"You talk like all the others," replied Phenice, sadly. "You too are making ricochets over the surface of the placid lake."

"Phenice, that's because I don't want to do you any harm, for, in order to tame you I could, if it pleased me, uproot a mountain, and with the arms of a giant, launch it over you, fallen as if from the sky. That mountain, Phenice, is my amour, which is threatening you. Yield, or I'll kill you!"

"Child," said Phenice, "you have more courage than I thought. Would you really be capable of killing me? I'm almost afraid—delectably! So be it, let the ordeal end; I'm yours."

Phenice got up and, pushing away the avidity of conquering hands, she undressed herself, slowly, with a singularly ironic and indecent calm. She acted as if she were alone, her fingers sure, her eyes cold and vague, indifferent to the gaze and pleas of her kneeling lover.

"You see," she said, finally, appearing naked—and truly similar to all other women—"you see, I told you so: it wasn't worth the trouble; the trouble I've had in undressing myself, the trouble you'll have in loving me. I have shoulders, arms breasts, knees; that makes a body only imperceptibly different from others. What pleasure do you have in gazing at this one rather than another, and what pleasure will you have in touching it when I permit you to do so? I'm neither more nor less than a woman, I'm mediocre, I'm an average and ordinary individuals—and that's why I've never allowed myself to be seen, except out of duty, and by eyes incapable of judging me. Well? I read in your eyes that you no longer love me; your arms no longer have the strength, nor the desire, to embrace me . . ."

"Phenice, absurd woman, you have the folly of scorn, but since I love you, I find you beautiful. You are the most beautiful of all women, Phenice; you are the only beauty that I desire. You are *the* woman . . ."

". . . My poor lover," said Phenice, resuming the interrupted speech, "I am indeed '*the* woman,' since I am a woman, that that is the *je ne sais quoi*, and that is why I have so many aspirants to my lips. Also know this: what I scorn in myself is the animality of the male, which has made me what I am: an animal."

Floriberte

THEY were talking, sitting on the edge of the water. Floriberte spoke with an ironic harshness.

"You want to take me away from all this," she said, indicating the meadows, the woods, the lake populated by swans, the old gray manor, one tower of which, still proud, proclaimed its ancient destiny, "all of this, all my animals, all my trees, all my grass! Is your soul, then, a landscape more beautiful than this one, with an older forest, a purer lake, softer and greener grass? Are there black swans and white swans in your heart? I'll never know; I don't want to go into it; I'm afraid of being duped and only finding an arid plateau, heather and dry grass—to which your ardent amour is perfectly capable of setting fire. I'd rather feed my swans."

And he, resolute but submissive, responded to Floriberte with amorous stupidities, which amused the young woman and made her think. In replying, she put a doubt in the place of the brutal negation; then, she suddenly perceived that, lifted up by a movement that was perhaps not unconscious, her dress had allowed a little of her leg to be seen, above the ankle.

Floriberte was one of those young women of breeding and blood in whom pride contends with sensuality. She would have given herself voluptuously to a lover, even a passer-by, had she not been stopped on the threshold of the possible realization by the sentiment that such a gift was truly too precious, and that one does not dilapidate a royal treasure thus. Pride incited her to malice and sensuality to complaisance; vanquished, Floriberte might become a mistress devoted to amour, but it was difficult to vanquish her, for her heart was hard.

Brought up alone and in liberty among inferiors, she was initially scornful of any stranger, capable of hating him if he attempted to put a hand on her independence; only the man who was conversing with her at present, at the water's edge, had obtained the grace of being heard. As it was necessary to marry, she had consented to marry him, but not to love him—and it was the latter issue, not the former that Floriberte and her fiancé were debating under the anxious gazes of the great swan.

Floriberte also said: "When I belong to you, my dear, you'll possess a woman whose corporeal beauty will dissipate, I hope, the vague sentimental aspirations with which you're imbued, like the mists of a matinal landscape. Don't render yourself ridiculous; don't destroy the physical attraction that might attach me to you; remember that I'm only enchained by a thread, and that I am capable of breaking iron fetters."

She lay back insolently, stretching herself out entirely on her back in order to pluck a leaf from the branches of a willow that were dangling behind her—but she sat up again rapidly, having heard the great white swan flap its wings.

"Let's get away!" she said, suddenly, her face pale and her eyes fearful.

※

Floriberte was married; but in the evening she was absent from the nuptial chamber.

She had gone out, having rapidly changed her dress, and she was walking alongside the lake, pensively, sad at having signed a promise the realization of which had become inevitable. Now it was no longer a matter of words but deeds; the discussion at the water's edge was about to materialize; and it seemed to Floriberte that a sort of crime was in preparation, an adultery worse than any other, and that she, who was habituated to scorn everything, no longer scorned anything as much as herself.

She walked along the shore of the slumbering lake; the swans were asleep in the reeds.

She was afraid, in thinking about the swans, those marvelous creatures that she loved, of the great white swan, her innocent lover, both of them, Floriberte and the pure bird, born on the same day! They had enjoyed so much together, both children, and they had said so many things to one another on the edge of the lake, while he stretched toward the young girl's hands his head with golden eyes, curving his flexible neck along her legs.

A truly absurd amour, but which no mythology had inspired, all Floriberte's tenderness had been devoted to her swan; her heart beat with emotion as she caressed his plumage and down, and when the handsome beast ate from her hand, she felt a pleasure of indescribable fraternity.

All sensual dreams were appeased in her in company with her swan, and her imagination, which was not corrupted, only requested a chaste pleasure from the bird's caresses.

She was afraid in thinking about the great white swan asleep amid the reeds; she was also afraid in picturing the empty bedroom where the sin, at this hour, might have been accomplished. Then, in order to beg his pardon, she searched for the great white swan amid the reeds; but the lake was vast, she searched poorly and it was pitch dark; she did not find him.

Fallen in the damp grass, she wept nervously, twisting her arms, prey to a strange crisis; but when she had wept abundantly, her pride returned to her, with the consciousness of her folly, and, resigned to the forgetfulness of puerile amours, she got up and went back inside, explaining her flight as a caprice, a desire for supreme solitude.

※

The next day, sensuality had been definitely awakened in Floriberte, and pride had limited her scorn. However, and as she had sworn, she never loved her husband with the tenderness of her heart; everything in her that had departed from sentiment she had lavished on the swans as candid as angels; a man evoked other desires for her, and realized other pleasures.

Floriberte never went to the edge of the lake any longer; she was afraid of the reproaches and the sadness of the great white swan.

Rosule

"WELL, Monsieur," said Rosule, "I've reflected. You can pay court to me, but I warn you that . . ."

She went into a corner to look for a large doll abandoned there for many weeks.

". . . If, after having conquered me, you don't realize all the promises of joy of which you've recited the rosary to me, and the nacreous beads of which I've counted carefully, I'll break you like this . . ."

Dryly, and without anger, she smashed the head of the doll against one of the iron chimeras that kept watch pensively under the high mantelpiece.

The porcelain head was shattered into little pieces, and Irenion could not help smiling at such childishness—but the two iron chimeras had mysterious reasons for remaining grave.

Then Rosule and Irenion, without saying anything more, went out into the gardens, which were embellished by the setting sun.

While they walked along a path planted with dahlias, Rosule appeared scarcely taller than the stems of the large frilly flowers, but she raised her head, from which an attached veil fell back over her shoulders; she marched erect, serious and imperious, and she was truly a young princess; Irenion resembled a giant set to guard her by a good fay.

There was a stream to cross, which seemed a river to Rosule. Irenion took her in his arms and strode over the water.

"You're tall and you're strong, Irenion," said Rosule, "but I'm wicked; because of my malice, I'm stronger and taller than you."

"Rosule," said Irenion, "little rose, you think that you're poisonous, but you're only perfumed."

Rosule could not help smiling, but, like the iron chimeras, the tall dahlias remained grave, and their heavy curly heads leaned over, ever motionless in the pure air.

They arrived at a place where there were large walnut trees charged with beautiful nuts, still prisoners in the shreds of their green matrix, but the branches were so high that Rosule thought: *No one will ever be able to reach them.*

Irenion only had to raise his arm in order to pick the beautiful nuts; then, stripped of their green matrix, he broke them like glass pearls and Rosule said: "Decidedly, Irenion, you're tall and strong; but I'm cunning, and by virtue of my cunning I'm stronger and taller than you."

Irenion did not dare make any response, for at the same moment, a great gust of wind passed by, which shook the old walnut-trees and strewed all the ripe nuts in the grass.

※

After their marriage, Rosule and Irenion lived in a large château surrounded by woods and meadows where one could walk for hours without ever passing along the same path twice or emerging from the domain. There, one felt like a king, master of the earth and the trees, the water and the grass, and almost of the wind and the clouds, but Rosule and Irenion had to attempt other pleasures first.

Rosule smiled; Irenion seemed happy; the nacreous beads of the rosary unfurled slowly and joyfully. One day, he dared to interrogate Rosule.

It was during a distracted stroll around a pond as large as a lake and as deep as the sea; the water was pure and blue; in the evening one could see the stars therein.

"Have I lied in my promises?" Irenion asked, simply.

Rosule made no reply.

"Rosule, little rose who think yourself poisonous and are only perfumed," said Irenion, softly, "have I lied in my promises?"

"Yes," replied Rosule.

"Rosule, it's you who are lying to yourself. You haven't said yes; I misheard. Rosule, did you really say yes?"

"Yes," said Rosule.

They remained silent for a few moments, and then Rosule said: "Imprudent man, who forces me to reflect and incline to one side a balance that would doubtless have oscillated forever, you're asking me whether your promises of joy have been realized? I don't know. You're asking me whether I'm happy? I know now that I wasn't, sufficiently for happiness to be inscribed in sure letters and clearly legible in my consciousness—but before your interrogation, I hadn't thought of deciphering the word perhaps in the process of being born, taking form and being gilded. You asked me a question; it was necessary to reply and I replied. Having nothing to say—nothing precise—I only desired to remain silent and keep my unformulated speech in limbo; you gave it life by speaking about it yourself.

"Imprudent man—mediocre, imprudent man too easily content, you don't know, then, that elect souls always lack something, something that neither amour, nor a man, nor God can give them. The only happiness attainable for intelligent beings is the unconsciousness of their woe. I ought to teach you that while there is still time, tall and strong man, while your giant brain is still palpitating within the powerful walls of its hard skull; I ought to teach you that, me, the feeble Rosule, the little poisonous rose.

"Do you suppose, then, Monsieur, that you have filled me with joys, like a measure of wheat, the grain of which one pours out until one reaches an iron rim? No, I have a soul, which is to say that I am insatiable; you were wrong to remind me of it. Think about what I said to you one day in autumn, passing over the stream and under the walnut trees, while the gardens were embellished by the glare of the setting sun—and also think about the death of my doll, whose head was made of porcelain."

※

Crouching on the edge of the pond, Rosule gazed at the singular eddies that troubled the pure blue water. Lifted up by the wind, the large veil with which she loved to envelop herself made two wings like the wings of the chimera that kept watch under the high mantelpiece, and her head, suddenly weighed down by the crime, leaned over, heavy and curly, like the head of a heavy and grave dahlia.

The Woman in Black

OF all the colors, shades and harmonies of hue, black definitely suited her. The reds and their substitutes pleased, in mirrors, her eyes anxious with joy, but a dissimulative night with enveloping folds reassured her fear of the truth. It was necessary to appear sad, since that was obligatory; that was the violent and secret will of a soul devoted to disguises.

Her soul! It was forbidden for her to glorify it in accordance with the line of the most delicate of poets: "my soul is an infanta in ceremonial dress,"[1] but—Albert Samain would pale at the parody—she could have sung to the nocturnal tune: "My soul is a ghost in ceremonial dress."

Her vocation was to appear unhappy, to pass through life like a groaning shade, to inspire pity, doubt and anxiety. She always gave the impression of taking flowers to an abandoned tomb, or coming back from one

---

1 "Mon âne est une infante," from *Au Jardin de l'infante* (1893), probably inspired by a Velasquez portrait of the Spanish infanta who became the French queen Marie-Thérèse, having been married to the future Louis XIV while both were children.

having wept over the sadness of premature destinies. If she smiled, it was the melancholy of a white rose in the moonlight, and if she laughed, people thought it was sarcasm.

In order to go at the first step all the way to the edge of the abyss, she first schemed to deceive God via the intermediary of a young priest whom she intoxicated with pure amour. She was then sixteen years old and enjoyed the novelty of no longer being a tomboy running around showing her legs; she showed her heart, an angelic object whose true place was on the display-cases of paradise, in God's museum.

The young priest handled such a precious trinket with infinite precaution and anointed it with perfumes, tears and benedictions. In giving her heart to God, she said to the young priest: "What a sacrifice I'm making you, my friend."

That lasted two years. She said that she was dead to the world, ready to immolate her hair, her flesh and her liberty; then, when her mother had wept a great deal, when she thought she had tortured all those who loved her cruelly enough, she pretended to yield to so much affliction and renounced depositing her heart in the glass cases of the celestial Jerusalem.

It was in that epoch that she adopted the dolorous black dresses that reminded her of her first widowhood and her first lie.

Then people were occupied with marrying her. Two suitors were admitted to make graces around the precocious inconsolable. One of them seduced her immediately with his bounty of a creature of the good

God, but she was capable of letting nothing show and offering to the other, and only to the other, the moonlight of her melancholy smile and the dubious grace of her distracted caresses.

How carefully she martyrized him, the worthy fellow, who only wanted to subjugate himself to all the whims of the incomprehensible virgin! Having understood that he was in love, she understood that he would suffer, without complaint, like an elect victim, proud of his election to dolor, and she did not spare him either dagger-thrusts or pin-pricks, much more painful because they are humiliating.

She dared to go as far as giving both hands to the other, to kiss, in front of him; as far as permitting suspect familiarities, such as allowing her hair to be caressed, under the pretext of games and floral crowns; and when the humble lover, very fearfully, offered the good will of his fingers, equally avid to touch and amuse their epidermis with the joy of contact, she said, dryly: "No, leave it; you're too clumsy."

However, having reflected for half a night, she resolved, not being audacious enough to lie to herself, quite simply to marry the man who loved her and whom she loved—but on that resolution, her diabolical nature put a frightful reservation.

It was one evening, in the great methodical garden where the enslaved trees admitted the supremacy of humankind. Straight pathways as broad as royal roads led from yews sculpted into porticoes to hornbeams whose curvature simulated grottoes and fashioned arbors. Framed by box-trees and lines of flowers, large bowling greens extended, like ponds, the mild calm of their velvet, and in the distance, and the end of all the pathways, beyond a pool of dead water, there was an almost unkempt wood that aristocrats disdained, except for hunting roe deer or poor girls dragging faggots of dead wood.

She invited her two suitors for a walk in that solitude. They arrived near the pool, where an old boat was dormant among the reeds. It was attached and taken to the foot of the steps; the beauty went down and entered it first.

"You take the oars first," she said to the one she was not going to marry. "I have confidence in you."

And when he had got into the boat and had taken the oars she said: "Get going!"

To the other, with a wave of the hand, she shouted, when the boat was already crushing the host of irises: "There's only room for two in my boat. Go around and come to meet us, or wait, for we'll come back."

She sang:

> *The boat flies,*
> *The boat runs,*
> *Like amour!*
> *The boat flies,*
> *The boat sleeps,*
> *Like death!*

Then, alone with the oarsman, she was seized by an amorous delirium and murmured, as if in ecstasy, the most passionate odes and the most languorous sonnets.

She disembarked without touching the earth with anything but her back, for he took her in his arms and laid her down on the ground, amid the slumbering primroses, in the shade and the peace of the silent forest.

Without saying anything, and as if merely astonished, she welcomed the first gestures and the first kisses, and then, sure of being vanquished, she simulated a furious revolt, but which eased gradually into tenderness and to free and absolute donation; however, she murmured, in the voice of a victim: "What a sacrifice I'm making you, my friend!"

They returned to the boat and she experienced a great secret joy in such a fine lie, for, having made a tour of the pool, the man whom she loved advanced, skirting the edge of the lake, which he had not crossed.

She went toward him, saying: "How frightened I was, merely for having touched the edge of the wood, merely for having set foot on the strip of shadow separating the wood from the rest of the world. Row me back into the garden, you, into the garden, into the garden! He can go around, in his turn."

"But three can easily fit into the boat," said the man who was returning from the forest.

"Three in the boat?" she said. "Why not? Let's go, we'll be three in the boat."

A few weeks later, she married the man whom she had chosen for that role from the very beginning, and, draped in the night of her lie, she entered into marriage as one inaugurates an adultery, murmuring in the touching voice of a victim: "What a sacrifice I'm making you, my friend!"

Intact

SHE came from a family of touching and quasi-symbolic mediocrity. Her father was a professor of the sixth at a small provincial college, and her mother, under the auspices of the university, kept a poor stationer's shop, where one found pencils, pens, lined paper, intellectual periodicals and images d'Épinal. For love of holy mythology her father gave her the singular name of Adonise, and it required the authority of a professor of rhetoric, an old paganized priest, to have such syllables inscribed in the sacred repository of the civil estate.

Adonise, in growing up, became the joy of the humble shop. As soon as she was eight years old she had acquired a perfect knowledge of all the varieties of metallic pens introduced into the town of Bayeux; apart from the death's-head, which she praised with the aid of a subtle discourse, she knew the lance, the gauloise, the lightning, the diamond and all the shades of Blanzys and Mitchells,[1] gave her opinion and offered

---

[1] Steel nibs for nineteenth-century pens were often oblique, and sometimes rounded, shaped to aid in the construction of broad

direct advice: "I know your handwriting, you need the lance." She wrote, in any case, with artistry, and her practice notebooks were the pride of the schoolmistress, dear Sister Bénévole.

In another genre of ideas Adonise was also unrivaled. Only the director of the honorable Maison Pellerin was as precisely up-to-date with the work of the worthy artists of Épinal.[1] Adonise, a living repertory, could recite without hesitation some three hundred titles of those lovable placards, and not only the familiar stories like "Prince Grésil" or "The Feline Fay," but extraordinary inventions such as "Alina and her Three Ducklings," "Paul; or How he Became a Millionaire," "Alice; or The Conseqences of a Lie" and many others, which Adonise could not name without emotion. "The Story of Prince Charming," for example, which had made her little heart beat faster

However, when she had made her first communion, the professor undertook to give her a truly serious education more in keeping with the destiny of the heiress of an esteemed pedagogue. Mythology seemed to him, from the outset, to be indispensable; he considered such a study to be the preface to all books, like the

---

and narrow strokes, the basis of the almost-lost art of calligraphy. One of the leading French manufacturers of varied nibs was the firm of Gilbert et Blanzy, and one of the leading English manufacturers was William Mitchell.

1 Jean-Charles Pellerin founded the Imagerie d'Épinal, which produced famous printed cards bearing a colored picture and a text is prose or verse, in 1796. For a century and more they were a popular wall decoration for poor people, especially children, and an important stock-in-trade for colporteurs.

portico under which it was necessary to pass in order to penetrate into the Temple of Taste. Adonise was illuminated with the science of Père de Jouvency, of the Society of Jesus,[1] who taught her the adventures of the thundering god, the labors of Hercules, and several other anecdotes that she judged less amusing and far less instructive than Petit Poucet.

Of all the oddities catalogued seriously by the old Jesuit, she only understood a little of the story of Diana, hunting wild boar and scorning men. Hunting wild boar must be an amusing occupation, and as for men, they appeared far inferior to the princes that Monsieur Pellerin dressed in such elegant doublets and such gracious plumed caps.

They had reached the demigods, the giants such as Briareus, and the bandits, such as Procrustes, when the professor died suddenly, while explaining devotedly how Romulus suckled, and not in vain, the nipples of a she-wolf. Adonise was then thirteen; she learned dressmaking, without neglecting calligraphy. The latter science, the most estimable and useful of all, was the salvation of the charming Adonise. As soon as she had attained the age required by the universitarian canons, she received a commission to teach handwriting to an amiable assembly of little cretins incapable of penetrating the secrets and assimilating the recipes of Brard and Saint-Omer,[2] the glories of the French school.

---

1 The Jesuit schoolteacher Joseph de Jouvency, or Jouvancy (1643-1719) produced a great many bowdlerized translations of Greek and Latin authors for use in French schools.

2 These two names are given in this formulation by Gustave Flaubert, George Sand and others, but an oft-quoted letter from

Adonise taught handwriting, executed accomplished models, rebuked little fingers stained with ink, distributed diplomas in calligraphy—and grew old.

She grew old without perceiving it, and without regrets. The smile of men had never moved her; it was deformed, by comparison with the precious simpers of the princes of Épinal. Their tender words—she had heard very few—were a barbaric and ludicrous jargon compared with the tender words with which the king disguised as a shepherd amused the shepherdess. She was conscious of living in an inferior, and even humiliating, world, and "all that" left her indifferent.

However, it happened one day—she was then thirty—that words pronounced in the pulpit by a very handsome Dominican troubled the pure blue lake on which her infantile heart sailed. The monk in question, of an exquisite modernity and a trifle jesuitical, attracted souls to him by intoxicating them with bitterness; he proclaimed the sadness of solitaries, the horror of the abandoned, and, perhaps according to the Admirable Ruysbroeck,[1] the pity that those who live without amour inspire.

Adonise was touched, but only slightly. That lasted two or three days; on the fourth, she abstained from the sermon of the seraphic Dominican, and reread in Jouvency the story of Diana, who hunted wild boar and scorned men.

Barbey d'Aureilly to Baudelaire fuses the two names into one as Brard Saint-Omer, who was allegedly the handwriting teacher of Joseph Prudhomme and Henri Monnier; opinions vary as to which version is correct.
1 The Flemish mystic Jan van Ruysbroeck (c1293-1381)

Then, she thought: "I am like Diana; no man has ever touched me."

She also thought in her virginal innocence, about calligraphy. *What's the point? And where's the pleasure? When one is married, one has children, but I have more than fifty, and very obedient, several of whom will give me the satisfaction . . .*

Then, ceasing to be cunning with herself, for if her innocence was real, her ignorance was not absolute, she murmured:

"Diana, Diana, what would you say if Adonise offered her lips to the avidity of a male, her breasts to the curiosity of a male, and her body to the brutality of a male? No! I'm intact, and I want to remain intact—and I too shall hunt wild boar in the Elysian wood and I shall scorn men. Oh, Diana, be my refuge and my recourse, protect me, love me, save me from those whose cowardly aggressive words want to attempt my integrity. You alone, and no other—not even Him, not even Jesus; Jesus is a man!"

From that day on, surprised people heard Adonise uttering strange words, but they thought that it was a remembrance of the profound science of which her father had disposed, and they smiled without comprehension. But in the concentration of her dreams, she was exalted; often, while the little girls were copying their models, she launched forth, bow in hand and quiver at her side, into the mysterious clearings of the Hyrcanian forests, and semi-naked, but chaste, and with her loins veiled, she commanded hounds and tamed wild beasts by means of the subtle power of her arrows.

She ended up becoming completely unhinged, people said, by virtue of forgetfulness of what was called the real world, in order to live out there, in the moonlight, under the old trees of the sacred wood, in order to run to the appeal of the conch, to triumph over the inferior forces of Nature, the Evil incarnate in sanguinary beasts.

Like her father, she died in a matter of hours, and, although a catholic daughter of the Church—she died sighing:

"Diana, O my mother, I am coming to you, I am worthy of you; no man has ever touched me; I am intact."

The Pensive Lady

SHE resembled closely enough one of those dark-haired virgin saints, arranged in an attitude of distracted melancholy. Her eyes, of a velvet blackness and a moist softness, always gave the impression of considering with astonishment a rare spectacle invisible to all other eyes; but she only ever gazed afterwards, when there was nothing more at which to gaze, at the beings and things that passed before her. Often, one could even speak to her, or touch her, without her perceiving it; she was one of those women who never know where they are, and never know where they are going.

She had married as if in a dream, less occupied with her husband than with the chimera whose flight she thought she was following, amid the possible landscapes and the skies open to her imagination. Throughout her life she wondered how she had become a woman, doubtless initiated while a wind of inconceivable perfumes enveloped her with unconscious delights.

As she also spoke very rarely, her soul always remained obscure, even for the benevolent wills most determined to force the door of the tabernacle, and it was said of Aline that she lived like a flower, or the Daphne of the *Metamorphoses*, mute and verdant.

A creature made to be loved, she was loved, like an icon, with a religious respect. People brought her the small presents that please simulacra, and her chapel, like a renowned sanctuary, was ornamented with garlands and ex-votos left by cured or consoled pilgrims. She was truly pacifying; her calm and her serenity soothed anxious hearts, and stained souls recovered their purity in being steeped in the dew of her soft black eyes.

By means of such gifts, she recognized love and compensated it; indiscreet desires stopped a few paces away from her, like superstitious brigands, and fell to their knees; the less fearful kissed the hem of her dress; not one of them had yet dared to lift it.

Every year, leaving her husband, a unique priest, to his affairs, the idol abandoned the sanctuary and went, a pilgrim in her turn, toward the dunes and the waves. Relatives welcomed her, proud of her imagistic beauty, and for months she ornamented the region, a Madonna on vacation.

She departed with her children, with the air of a Laure thinking about her Petrarch, the pensive Lady, and the train carried her away, unaware of landscapes, noises and the petty annoyances of travel. She arrived: the sea! The sea, fatherland of dreams! Aline, a living dream, found brethren among the melancholy pines rustling eternally in the sea breeze.

The dunes were her garden; all day long, she walked in the lukewarm sands, or, fatigued, lay down in the thin grass in the sheltered hollows. Violent or pacific, near or distant, murmurous or roaring, the sea sometimes frightened the pensive Lady, by obliging her to pay attention to it; the sea wanted her to gaze at it, the sea wanted her to listen to it, the sea forced Aline to emerge from her dream, the sea was jealous, the sea wanted to be loved; Aline was frightened and fled into the dunes; crouched in the sand, like an ant-lion, but innocent, she remained motionless for hours, smiling—smiling angelically—attracting to her by means of her breath the invisible reveries, tiny creatures, of which the air is full.

Aline was happy, for she was alone. No matter how scantly she felt them, contacts made her suffer, at least afterwards, by reaction; the idea that someone had just touched her, or even spoken to her, caused her, if not a pain, at least an embarrassment. In the street, the gazes of "impure passers-by" had sometimes given her, on days of nervousness, the impression of a net of dirty cords that she had to break in order to pass through; here, enveloped by solitude, she was not soiled or touched by the desires of any individual, and in the absolute absence of sensations, folded entirely upon herself, sure that no contrary fluid would come to trouble the pure current of her eternal dream, Aline rose up almost as high as ecstasy.

A woman made to be loved—but above all to be divined, closed under the stone veils of the cloister; doubtless destined for the most intoxicating amours! Not to act, not to speak; sometimes to sing; that is the ideal of more than one person; it was Aline's ideal; and her veritable vocation.

In her phases of solitary ecstasy, Aline sometimes sang; it was a sort of joyful lament emerging from unconscious lips, a rhythmic chant, like that of the sirens, over the respiration of the sea.

She sang, and a fisherman coming back, chased by the rising tide, heard the song of the siren, the joyful lament of the pensive Lady; astonished, he pricked up his ears, accustomed to perceive the slightest nuances of the song of the wind in the pines; he had never heard such a song—he, who knew all the songs of the sea, for whom the foolish sirens had inflated their lungs and broken their conches; he got his bearings, he searched, and in a hollow in the dunes, he perceived Aline.

She was lying on her back, scarcely clad; her light white dress scarcely made a mist over her limbs, and her upper body was affirmed, held by her folded arms. Aline was charming, and a true siren thus posed on the sand, like a delectable wreck borne there by a caprice of the wind; her black hair spread out like wrack, truly similar to the algal tresses of sirens. The fisherman, still damp with sea-water, approached the apparition and caressed it with his heavy hand.

Aline was still singing, departed in a dream, ecstatic, her eyes closed; the fisherman, with his heavy hand, took possession of the wreck. Aline was still singing; the fisherman kissed the siren on the shoulder respectfully, as he had seen the priest kiss the altar before the sacrifice, because he was emotional and religious before such a beauty. Aline was still singing; the fisherman completed his work—and he saw clearly that she was not a siren, for no siren allowed herself to be approached so closely, and none ever risked conceiving of a man.

Aline stopped singing; the pensive Lady awoke, shivering, got up, her mouth bitter from the kiss that had stopped on her lips the flight of her dream song.

The fisherman fled, frightened; she seized him by the hand; he obeyed and listened.

"Why have you stolen me? I belonged to one alone, and his chain was gentle to me because I did not feel its weight. To belong to one alone is still to be free, for that one can love her—which is to say, to assimilate her to himself, to dissolve her in himself... but you, stranger, you have weighed upon my heart with all your weight, you have bruised me, you have been my master; from this moment on I am your mistress. Come, we shall wash ourselves together of the crime you have made me commit. Do you hear the voice of the sea—the sea that I love and of which I am afraid? She is calling to us and advancing to meet us; come! Why have you stolen me? I am one whom one does not steal twice; I am the treasure that is animated, that agitates, that twists and coils like an invincible serpent around the neck of the thief; come!"

And the pensive Lady, awakened from her dream, rose up, terrible, inhuman, implacable, and, taking the fisherman by the hand, she went with him toward the sea, dragging him like a little child.

The pensive Lady went into the sea.

Melibea

PEOPLE wondered how a young woman so agreeable and so well-endowed had been able to wait, before being married, to the age of twenty-four, already heavy to bear for an ardent virgin. Several reasons were whispered, and even spoken out loud: the parents were stupid, insupportable and of a rather dishonest reputation; the young woman was badly brought-up, disdainful, arrogant, bold, impertinent, and endowed with a gaze whose brightness, almost libertine, frightened the bravest and the most resigned. Then again, the ridiculousness of her name was insinuated: Melibea, frightful syllables that gave the impression of amours that were truly too Virgilian.[1]

All that was true, but it was even more true that Melibea remained unmarried by choice. She had not renounced marriage; ready to give herself, she was waiting for a romantic occasion: powerful arms that had

---

1 The reference is ironic because the "Melibee" in Virgil's *Eclogues* (borrowed by Chaucer in the *Canterbury Tales* and Spenser in *The Faerie Queene*) is a male shepherd who sings the praises of the pastoral frame of mind.

proved their strength, a raised sword dripping blood, a gladiatorial foot crushing the breast of an agonizing adversary.

Her sentimentality was cruel even in dreams. As others fantasized about boats carrying away enlaced lovers and silken ladders on which adroit Romeos were swinging, she liked to imagine carnage and see herself, as night fell over a battlefield, lying in bloodstained grass, proudly smiling in the brutal embrace of the conqueror.

Imaginations as abominable and puerile sometimes made her ashamed, however, and she consented to kiss the hands of a metaphorical conqueror, a peaceful athlete. Fundamentally, she wanted above all to be won like a prize, to be awarded like a crown. An object as remarkable as Melibea could not belong to just anyone; it must be "by right of conquest."

Oh, how she would have loved those tourneys in which two knights fought, often to the death, and what anxiety there would be in wondering which would die and which would be her master. Often, she had thought of organizing some ferocious duel between her suitors, but imagination failed her and, for want of experience, her inventions only ended in minuscule quarrels, soon appeased.

However, the fervor of her blood pressed her to conclude; obscurely, she foresaw the moment when she would become the almost voluntary prey of a clever audacity—and that is what happened.

Only laureates were received in the house, award-winning men who had the right, like prize cattle, to wear floating ribbons and rosettes of gilded paper. The man who curbed the proud Melibea under his knee was, therefore, a laureate, but of the most mediocre species, a derisory and asinine laureate, a laureate in regard to the genre of whose triumphs it was necessary, for decency's sake, to keep quiet; a laureate, in sum, of neutered literature and castrated art.

That unscrupulous young man undertook the seduction of Melibea by means of the game of reticence. He told her impassioning stories that he stopped dead, saying: "When you've married me, you'll know the rest." Or he presented marriage as an immeasurable abyss of felicities, an infinite ocean of incessantly renewed delights, and he insinuated that the majority of divorces were caused by the inaptitude of certain individuals to support excessive pleasures, joys whose amplitude went as far as exquisite dolor. He explained all that in terms much more gallant and much less veiled, so well that Melibea ended up confiding to him the care of guiding her to paradise.

They were married, but the gates of heaven scarcely opened. Melibea perceived the splendors of the luminous city, but for the interval of a second, and night fell again upon her heart. She demanded explanations; she was always given the same ones. She got annoyed; there was complete darkness, without lightning. Feeling duped and betrayed, she abandoned herself to the painful caresses of despair; she wept and wailed, but in vain, for the magic word was lacking to which the obstinacy of the gates of Heaven yields.

She had failed to follow her nature; she had mistaken the path. Then Melibea returned to her former dreams, of bloody arms that opened to embrace the conquered woman, and her husband horrified her.

Fortunately, he was jealous. In that discovery, Melibea experienced some joy, for a woman of her character always finds means of getting rid of a jealous husband. Her plan was as simple as her hopes were vast and complicated, for she intended to utilize that futile husband very seriously and to make his disappearance serve simultaneously for the realization of the dream of all her youthful sentimentality.

She had to hand the combatant who was to die, the gladiator whose breast was to be crushed by the foot of a pitiless adversary; it only remained to find the adversary—the conqueror!

It required a strong and clever man, and that the man in question become sufficiently amorous to be imprudent; it required an adventure such that her husband would be obliged to fight; it required, not only an evident commencement of adultery, but also a public insult, a premeditated offense.

With a diabolical skill, she organized the entire affair. A friend of her husband was the chosen partner and adversary; as Melibea was desirable, a few trivial advances reckoned with his amity. The rest was easy. When Melibea had gone for a walk three times with a stranger at dusk in the back streets of her quarter, under the hateful gazes of maids, on the fourth day her husband suddenly loomed up, emerging from a coaching entrance.

Everything happened appropriately, as discreetly as a street permits discretion; witnesses made a few reciprocal visits, and one morning, two small caravans met on a charming islet, enlivened by the first rays of dawn and birdsong.

What delightful moments you spent dreaming, O Melibea, and what delightful dreams, while the blades were clashing out there on the charming and cheerful islet! You followed in thought all the phases of the duel, and your thought saw everything: the feints, the recoils, the parries, and the serenity of the witnesses! You saw everything, but then an unexpected cloud enveloped your vision; you know that one of the two has been touched by death, but which?

Tragic uncertainty, O Melibea! Which? What if the one you have chosen to be defeated is going to return to you and say: "The other isn't coming back"? What if the husband you scorn surges forth before you, holding out his arms to you?

Which? Melibea tried not to think about it any longer. Upright, in a pose of joyful resignation, she awaited her master, the man who would have conquered her by blood, the one who would give her the joy of belonging to a conqueror.

The door opened. Her husband came in, saying: "A man has died."

Then Melibea fell to her knees, and her criminally beautiful eyes informed the sad gladiator of the admiration of the woman, the desire of the female and the submission of the slave.

The Virgin of the Plaster Casts

DORY had been, until the age of twenty-five, the purest virgin, so pure that she did not even know what purity was. An entirely white and stainless lamb, her candor was not a merit; she was candid by nature and by estate, like lilies, snow and salt.

Without losing anything of her innocence she could look at nudity, even her own; neither the beauty of statues nor her own informed her of the usage of beauty. In her father's workshop—he was a skillful molder and sculptor's assistant—she wandered with impunity among the torsos, abdomens, hips, legs and sex organs, and she sold to all comers torsos, abdomens, hips, legs, entire goddesses or complete heroes. Gladly, without modesty and without blushes, she gave her opinion, advising the loins of the Medici Venus, the knees of the Diana of Gabii, the belly of the cracked Apollo and the loins of the hermaphrodite Bacchus.

Her taste was as reliable as her esthetic science, and at the annual exhibitions every conscientious sculptor collected Dory's opinion deferentially. She had posed once—or, rather, she had consented to allow herself to be modeled standing, but the work displeased her, the artist, in her view, not having rendered with exactitude the special character of her beauty, which was flexibility and grace. She never lent herself to a further experiment, and contented herself with having molded, very carefully, several parts of her body: the shoulders, the breasts and the legs, including the knees.

She esteemed those fragments of herself the equal of the most decisive masterpieces, although she was the first to say that a mold from life produces results more curious than artistic; but they were truly beautiful specimens of nature, and they took their place in the molder's shop, hung from the ceiling amid the host of shoulders and legs. Dory sold them, admitting their origin, and she sold a great many—and Dory's plaster breast received many kisses from many mouths.

She had never wanted to marry. In all innocence, she was self-sufficient, and in any case, no carnal desire fomented in the chastity of her body, so marvelously perfect. Marriage, for her, was what she saw in the street: a deformed belly poorly dissimulated under naïve pleats, the belly of a ruminant, a monstrosity analogous to that of hunchbacks, doubtless more benign, since it had a term, but just as afflicting, and even more humiliating. Her love of beauty, of the pure line, was so absolute and so sensible that she truly suffered as soon as, outside her plaster museum, she walked among the abominable creatures falsely named women who cluttered the sidewalks with their gaits of articulated mannequins.

She dreamed then, in order to distract herself, of a land where beauty walked free, where noble human animality, liberated from morality, fashion and modesty, was naked and glorious. Naïvely, she imagined a people of statues, without suspecting the absurdity of such a dream and without thinking that the ugliest garment is almost always less ugly than the body that wears it. Nor did she suspect the inconveniences of such mores, and how shocking her love of the line would be to them, for desire breaks proportions and breaks norms; but, habituated to the purity of her plasters, instructed by their esthetic, protected by their coldness, she pursued her innocent imagination of a humankind in conformity with the principles of Jean Cousin[1] and, weary of her sad walks, returned to the molder's shop with the joy of an angel reentering paradise.

All the rooms of the apartment, not only the shop and the workshop, were full of arms, legs and torsos. That florescence of limbs and fragments had even invaded her bedroom, where a few pieces that were rare or problematic in sale had been installed, such as the ephebe who symbolizes Eternal Repose, an underappreciated work, and the Callipygian Venus, a collector's item that no provincial museum or school dared to buy. Dory, by contrast, loved the pure Callipygian

---

[1] The painter, engraver and geometer Jean Cousin (c1500-c1590) applied his mathematical expertise to painting techniques in a book on perspective published in 1560; it was followed by a book on anatomy and portraiture probably written by his similarly-named son (c1522-1595), the initial publication of which is uncertain, but which became celebrated in the seventeenth century, when it was reprinted many times.

very much, whom she only reproached for her movement of coquetry, and it was pleasant for her to undress in the presence of such an amiable goddess and to borrow in sleep from the ephebe of Eternal Repose the grace of his immortal slumber and the attitude of his divine ennui.

As for Dory's father, an Italian living in London who had become taciturn, he made molds and did not know anything else.

Now, it happened that a rather singular ephebe—Dory called young men ephebes—came into the shop one day, looked at the plasters, looked at Dory, did not buy anything and left without opening his mouth.

Dory was as discreet as she was indifferent; she did not importune the ephebe with any offer or any question, and limited herself to following him in his journey through the plaster stalactites and opening the door for him when he had completed his exploration. Nevertheless, she found his behavior a little strange, and on reflection, judged herself almost offended. He had scarcely saluted her as he entered and left. The shop was a museum, to be sure, but not a public museum, and the guardian had a right to more than a glance, to a word.

In himself, the ephebe scarcely interested her; he was a thin individual, slightly deformed in one shoulder, one leg seemingly weaker than the other, too pale and too blond, with an unhealthy and timid appearance. Such a creature was certainly not made to move Dory's esthetic soul—and yet she surprised herself, the following day, thinking about the stranger and excusing his impoliteness. He was, she thought, an unfortunate fellow afflicted by an excessive timidity. He was paltry, but certainly intelligent and she would gladly have exchanged with him a few of the callistic aphorisms of which her heart was full.[1]

The opportunity was given to her, for the stranger returned and showed himself less timid. He was a melancholy Englishman who collected all the plaster casts that could be procured on the surface of the earth. He had gathered countless quantities of them, populating a series of sheds in the vicinity of London as long as five or six Louvres, and he had come to see whether he might encounter in the shop some unusual piece that had escaped him thus far. Naturally, Dory showed him the plaster fragments of her own beauty, and the Englishman, intoxicated by joy at such a discovery, immediately bought two shoulders, two breasts and two legs, the beauty and finesse of which he praised; he had healthy ideas in matters of art.

Meanwhile, Dory took pleasure in the company of such an extraordinary ephebe; she sensed a spiritual brother, a soul that, like hers, was only nourished by esthetics, and soon, by virtue of an aberration unique in her life, she began to love that frail framework, that meager flesh, those shrunken forms—or rather, she unconsciously made an abstraction of all the flaws of the lame Apollo in order better to enjoy the delicacy of his intelligence and the flame of his eyes.

---

1 The tern "callistic" has almost dropped out of usage now, but it figures significantly in the philosophy of Plato as the study of beauty, as distinguished from the study of art (aesthetics).

He was witty when he deigned to enter into conversation, and he had the most beautiful eyes in the world; wit and beautiful eyes were so new to the virgin of the plaster casts that she was seduced. The chaste, pure, esthetic Dory was in love.

Then she lived among her stalactites hours even sweeter than in the past. She found a new grace in the statues and the hanging limbs, and in taking inventory with her dear lover of all those dead things she felt an infinite joy in being alive. Gradually, an entirely new soul had germinated and blossomed within her; one day, when her friend kissed her hand, she understood modesty, and one day, when her friend took her gently in his arms, she understood life.

It was a Dory very different from the old one, almost tender—and almost impure, since she was in love.

But she was only loved by the caprice of a temporary ennui, and so little desired that the desire went away without having requested from that virginity the serious sacrifice of its essence. The young monomaniac disappeared unexpectedly and Dory, who had to wait for him eternally, never heard any further mention of him.

In the shop with the plaster pendants, amid the legs, the abdomens, the torsos and the shoulders, Dory wept, astonished by her tears, simultaneously sad and humiliated by an amour for which she had not wished and an abandonment that her pride had not anticipated.

And until the years of her physical decadence, and beyond, Dory lived internally on a pale memory and an illusory desire. No other amour consoled her for that first and unique disappointment; for, in accordance with very obscure laws, she must have been punished, after having loved beauty, for having been infidel to the cruel goddess; and it was necessary for Dory, the innocent and proud adorer of the androgyne Apollo, to mourn the disdain of a deformed passer-by.

A Virgin's Adventure

THE confession—not the confidence—that I'm going to make to you, my friend, is one that ought to be complete, without reticence, absolute; no detail will therefore be spared your modesty; you will blush, you will weep, perhaps you will cry—but you will listen, because it is necessary that a human creature knows my adventure, in order to repeat it to God.

You know that I often return in the evening, alone from Vassy to Chaumont, by the last train. I've spent the day with our dear Bergerette, and when we separate, at eleven o'clock, I'm taken to the station, put into a compartment, and I sleep until the time comes to fall into the arms of my father, who waits for me on the platform, and always divines the door that it's necessary to open.

That train, it's said, runs for me alone, or almost. It only brings back to Chaumont a few merchants who have chanced to be in Vassy on business—others say their amours. Oh, my dear, how can I write such a word, now that I know what it signifies? But those good people assemble on the same banquettes, and I think that for three years, I always traveled alone at that hour.

All that is in order for you to know that there was no premeditation in my crime, and to enable you to understand that my adventure could not have been organized or planned, so that you will believe that only a diabolical fatality could have driven me to commit an action that, thus far, like you, like all our pure and honest friends, I had always reproved as much as murder—or suicide.

So, I was thrust into the carriage. We were late and the train was already in motion, so that I only boarded by grace and because I am, for that train, a sort of reason for existence, a sort of sacred consignment. We had already traveled some distance when, having recovered from my emotion, I perceived in the opposite corner a man wrapped up in blankets.

I must tell you that, immediately, fulgurantly, without any resistance of my conscience, I was gripped, seized and carried away by the mad desire—mad, but absolute and ineluctable—to be possessed by that man. Me, a virgin! The sole reflection that I made was that I had nothing to fear, and all the time before me, since the journey to Vassy, without stopping, lasts exactly an hour; as soon as I arrived I would leap down and I would disappear.

The summons was imperious. I sensed a singular and unknown warmth in my face, in my breast and—I must tell you everything—in parts of my body that had never yet given me any dangerous anxieties. It was as if I were drunk, with the intoxication incited by one glass of champagne too many—no, these petty intoxications of young women are nothing, nothing; I was subject not to a temptation but to an irrefutable commandment.

I was neither stupid nor gauche, and while a chorus of almost comminatory voices cried within me: "Yes! Yes!" I observed.

The man was fairly young, strong, not without elegance—all that was necessary for the murder, for the violation, that I was about to demand. He stirred, changed position, woken up by my appearance and my agitation, for my heels, by virtue of a singular nervous twitch, were striking the floor rhythmically. Soon, he loosened his blankets, adjusted his little traveling cap, and looked at me. I was afraid that he might read my eyes as in an alphabet, a missal with enormous letters; I was afraid that he might scorn too easy a prey. But I was a truly beautiful prey, an ineluctable prey, and—since he required it—I looked at him in my turn. That was all I did. No, I did more, O diabolism of innocence and perversity of instinct! I lifted my dress slightly, as if to drape it around my legs, and I adopted a weary and insolent pose, the pose of a woman who is waiting and cannot wait.

Meanwhile, I began trembling; I was shivering as at the first moment of a cold bath, and the rhythm of my heels accelerated in accordance with a disquieting rapidity.

He leaned toward me and said: "Oh, how you're trembling! Let me wrap you in this blanket . . ."

His voice was soft. I replied affirmatively with an equal softness. He stood up and brought me all his blankets. I was still trembling, and fearfully; my eyes were wild; I didn't move; my arms were heavy and my hands indecisive. He wrapped me up maternally, from the feet to the neck, tucking me in and patting me like a child being put to bed.

I believe that I really was cold; that did me good, and I smiled.

Then he was emboldened, continuing to pat me gently and needlessly, smoothing and pressing the blankets along my legs and my hips.

I smiled seriously; I smiled as a furnace smiles.

Then he became even bolder. He leaned his head over me to the point of touching my hair, and, doubtless not daring to say any more, he asked: "Is that better?"

I responded with a feeble "yes," and—oh, my friend, can you read this?—mechanically, I believe, without deliberation, without will, but in full consciousness of my action, with joy, I let my knee move sideways to collide with his. He put his hand on my knee, he leaned on it, he persisted; I relaxed instead of resisting—and then he dared everything!

I was dying of desire, of lust. Yes, my friend, without budging, without closing my eyes, still smiling, I allowed myself to be taken in detail, inch by inch, and delectably! He did what he wanted, and everything he wanted, I wanted; I lent myself, I gave myself, I offered myself—and I rose up to a summit of vertiginous voluptuousness!

Yes, I allowed myself to be taken—all the way! Yes, and I took myself, shamelessly; I kissed his lips, I clasped those random shoulders, and I screamed my dishonor!

I was a happy beast.

As he looked at me conceitedly—I thought—or with ennui or fatigue, the arrival whistle sounded. I got up.

He said: "I'm going all the way to Merville, but . . ."

"No, let me go and continue. Only tell me your name."

He gave me his card. I just had time to secret it in my bodice, and the train stopped.

I said: "Not a word!"

He understood, and withdrew toward the other door. I leapt out and fell into my father's arms. My sister, who was with him, started to laugh as she looked at me. "How disheveled you are!"

I alleged that I had slept wrapped in my dress—and that was all, for was any suspicion possible? Oh, I shall be very tranquil if God, as I hope, as I wish, spares me the consequence of my crime!

And now, my friend, here I am, the next morning, and in this condition: ashamed and joyful, humiliated and satisfied. I know, I am, I live, a woman, like Psyche, by virtue of a man or a succubus? Oh, what does it matter, since it was one or the other, since I shall never see the initiator again—for, I swear, I burned the card without reading it. A recommencement, or merely the possibility of a recommencement, would have been no longer a crime but a depravity.

Perhaps I shall accomplish a vulgar destiny—and lie, if I marry—but at least my first step into the mystery will have been bold, incredible and diabolical . . . or divine! And if I don't take a second, I shall be fortunate even so.

Fortunate in my fall, yes, I repeat it, even though you might pale in fear or horror. I adore while blushing, but I adore the unknown, obscure and formidable Cause that lay me down under the embrace of a passer-by, and did that in the banality of a railway carriage polluted by all respirations, while the axles were creaking, while the wheels, biting the rails, rang like the hammers of a distant forge, while the train ran, crazier than my blood, toward the abyss, toward annihilation!

Tristane

TRISTANE went forth under the russet leaves that were flying away one by one and coming to fall at her feet. Autumn afflicted the great wood of beeches and oaks, but the belated oaks still had green crowns, and Tristane thought that life does not die without supreme reviviscences. She raised her head and saw that amid the white clouds, a blue river was shining with a soft pallor.

She was walking wrapped in an amazon dress, all black, although the neck was circled by a serpent of yellow fur, bare-headed, because she was at home; her unshakable coiffure defied the surprises of the wind, and her tresses, of a charming blonde, veiled the cares of her temples; her march was melancholy and slow, allowing her long dress to sweep the grass in which the last daisies were asleep.

That walk toward the latest lover now took her along paths planted with memories, wild rose-bushes and their bloody and bitter berries, which she plucked in passing, tearing her fingers thereon.

Oh, to be very small still, with all the mystery of the terrible forest before one's eyes, to be content with a fraternal caress and a frilly dress, and suddenly to want one of the flowers of the verge, to want the lips of a little scamp who grazes his legs climbing a tree in which an empty nest is trembling!

But Tristane commented on her first memory: "All the nests are empty. That young kiss, without the joy of theft and the joy of immodesty, would have been as insipid as a hedge mulberry—and when the same child, the following year, returned my caress, his eyes ardent and his gestures insolent, I only experienced the pleasure of wrongdoing, the delights of the illicit and the hidden."

Afterwards, grave people ornamented with ribbons or embroideries had permitted her to sleep with a man, permitted and even commanded it. They said with menacing smiles: "Your duty is to sleep with that man henceforth, and with him alone."

Throughout the first night, and many other nights as well, Tristane had thought about those pious stories in which virgins are delivered to expert and inventive torturers—then, habituated to the torture, she slept resigned, but thoroughly bruised by the duty.

She only quivered, eventually, under a strange gaze; rediscovered, as fresh and more blooming, the joys of the illicit and the hidden enabled her to believe, for a few days, in the beauty of life; faded, she collected others, and yet others; but the new flowers withered ever more rapidly, and Tristane had less courage to extend her hand toward the disillusionment of roses.

Tristane looked behind her and saw a path unfurling into the distance, like the path strewn with petals that was once offered to the Holy Sacrament.

"So many broken flowers, and no perfume remains to me, either on my fingers or in my heart!"

Once again, she wanted to become very small, in order to retread, more carefully, the route traveled in vain, in order better to choose among the wild roses and the dahlias, *for*, she thought, *I have certainly passed, without seeing them, alongside the most flowery and the most odorous branches.*

"No. What would be the point? I'd deceive myself again, I'd trample the same grass, advance my hand toward the same errors, open my arms to the same phantoms, with the same innocence in my gestures and in my eyes. Now, I know. I know how it is necessary to take and how it is necessary to give. I'm not at the end of my road; there's still a temporary altar before the chapel."

※

Tristan, therefore, went toward the latest lover.

He came from far away and he was far away, but she saw him surging from hill to hill, ablaze like a furnace and as bright as a beacon; those apparent lights guided Tristane and soothed her oin her journey.

She no longer turned her head to look behind her; the images of the past were extinguished successively, little lamp blown out by the patrol; alone, in the midst of a great night, Tristane walked courageously toward the light surging from hill to hill.

It was night, truly, in the silent forest; Tristane was scared by the sound of her footsteps crushing the dead leaves; then she crouched down at the foot of a tree and waited, her eyes fixed on the distant glow.

As soon as Tristane was sitting at the foot of the tree, the forest went to sleep more profoundly, without sighs and without dreams, buried in the delights of oblivion; and Tristane went to sleep too, for slumber is stronger than amour.

Tristane went to sleep at the moment when a belated traveler was passing by, making anxious gestures, plunging attentive glances into the shadows; he inclined his head from side to side, his ears pricked, and he often stopped in order to listen and look harder; but Tristane, crumpled at the foot of the tree, seemed as vague and as black as a clump of furze or a clump of heather.

He shouted: "Tristane!"

The voice plunged into the shadow and brought no response; then the traveler retraced his steps, brushing past Tristane again without recognizing her; eventually, he lay down in the dead leaves and he too went to sleep amid the silent trees.

Daylight woke them up; they got up and drew away.

I've been happy in a dream, thought the traveler.

O my latest lover, thought Tristane, *what a night of obscure and profound delights! You've finally given me the plenitude of the joys of amour. I've been happy in a dream.*

Part Three:

Anecdotes

The Bad Monk

It is not necessary to live, but it is necessary to think.

Leibniz

THE man who was already called "the monk," because of his chaste life and his bitter speech, became one, really and forever, in his thirty-fifth year. After long and enervating conversations with a singular poet, who had sketched conscientious novitiates in all the monasteries in France, he decided on a Trappist monastery, and for that of Soligny, made illustrious by Rancé,[1] even more rigid and more mysterious than all the others.

He believed that he had a special entitlement to complain of life, of women who had not loved him, of men who had not understood him, of things whose hostility had loomed up like a line of reefs between him and his desire every time he had launched his skiff on the sea, every time he had set his sail toward Thule or Atlantis.

---

1 Armand-Jean de Bouthillier de Rancé (1626-1700) was the founder and abbot of the monastery of La Trappe at Soligny, which gave its name to the Trappist offshoot of the Cistercians.

In truth, he had scarcely manifested anything but whims, very petty desires as fragile as soap bubbles, as pretty and as vain. He was not even one of those whom Fourier,[1] the inventor of the Four Movements and of amusing psychology, calls "commencers"; he did not even commence, always remaining within the boundary of the departure. Capable of letting himself go and obeying an impulse, like a bell, he ceased to ring as soon as the cord was released. One of his weaknesses was that of remaining where he was; he was always the last to leave a drawing room, a theater or a café; he had to be thrown out, always surprised that the "already" had sounded. Undoubtedly, he would have made an excellent stylite, and, perched on his column, he would never have thought of coming down from it.

His friend the poet, on the other hand, was the accomplished type of the inveterate commencer, ready to try anything, to taste everything, without ever emerging, except by accident, from the domain of the Church, which retained him with an obscure but ineradicable vocation. In the Middle Ages, in the thirteenth century, he would have been one of those gyrovague clerics, one of those "goliards" who went from abbey to abbey, transporting pious legends and scabrous songs, incapable of settling, of submitting irredeemably to a rule, amorous of new faces, unfamiliar locations, adventures, always on the move, convinced that one is only at ease where one is not.

---

1 The Utopian philosopher Charles Fourier (1772-1837), author of *Théorie des quatre movements et des destinées générales* (1808; tr. as *The Social Destiny of Man; or, Theory of the Four Movements*).

Alone, "the monk" would never have left. The poet set him on the road. Devoid of money but furnished with letters of credit, they went on foot, traveling like colporteurs, eating and sleeping in presbyteries, not always well received, but contriving by some mummery to conciliate ecclesiastical suspicion.

At La Trappe the abbot welcomed them, in accordance with the rule of the Order, with affability, remembering the constitution of Rancé, in which it is said of guests: *take care to treat them with so much charity that they have no reason to believe that they are a burden and that their visit is importunate.*

From the first day spent in the peace of silence they were equally seduced, and the poet resolved very firmly to undertake his seventh novitiate there.

He did not persevere for more than a month, and departed, leaving behind "the monk," who was not to emerge again, thus confirming, once more, the terrifying dictum of Pascal: *The will is never satisfied when it can do whatever it wishes, but satisfied as soon as it renounces desire.* In truth, his merit had not been very great, so mediocre was the quality of the will that he renounced. For him the rule was, on the contrary, a powerful principle of activity, and he did not take long to obey it mechanically, to march like a docile ewe among the flock.

After two years of novitiate, he was admitted to the profession; he pronounced the three great vows of poverty, chastity and obedience—and he felt that he was very happy.

Getting up at two o'clock in the morning, fasting until midday, singing in the choir, laboring in the fields, living on vegetables and fruits, sleeping on a board, and many other austerities were not long delayed in becoming part of his habits. In any case, the lack of nourishment and sleep soon induced a sort of torpor or daze from which he never awoke; at certain times, in the morning and evening, he seemed to be dead already, or at least no longer living any but a ghostly life, and he only recovered consciousness of himself in the fields, when he mowed the hay or harvested the wheat.

He did not experience the joys of the mystical life any more than the majority of his brethren, and less than the least of them, for he was neither devoted nor pious, nor even a Christian. Nevertheless he followed all the exercises scrupulously, delivered himself to the prescribed prayers and reading, and observed the rule in every detail, without zeal but without ill will. *Sedebit solitarius et tacebit.*[1] Silence was agreeable to him; what repose from the futile and tumultuous conversations in which he had once fatigued and used up his youth!

Only once was he moved, but as far as fear, by the frisson. It is customary, at La Trappe, that if a monk dies, his place in the refectory is respected for a month, and that the dead man's meals are served at that place. Now, it happened that his two neighbors died one after another, and for a month he was obliged to eat elbow to elbow with the absence of the two dead men. That

---

[1] The quotation is from the Vulgate version of *Lamentations* 3:28, rendered in the A.V. as "He sitteth alone and keepeth silence."

impression, very painful to him at first, was nevertheless salutary, by virtue of informing him that he was not yet sufficiently detached from life, since the contact of death was dolorous to him. A few meditations calmed him.

In any case, his turn came. He had been living there for thirty years; he was sixty-five years old: an age that is rarely surpassed at La Trappe monastery, and is not often attained. A great weakness gripped him; he sensed, as did everyone else, that it was the end, and he resigned himself to undergo the great ceremonial that accompanies the death-throes of Trappists.

In accordance with the rule, he was taken down into the chapel, and there laid upon a heap of straw in order to receive the last sacraments, surrounded by all the brethren. The abbot, in a violet stole, cross in hand, recited the prayers for the dying; the monks, on their knees, responded. When the prayers were complete, the abbot, seeing that he was bleak, and his eyes were glazed, leaned over him and exhorted him.

"Speak, my friend," he said, in a low voice. "Sins have often been seen here retained until death, which only emerge from the mouth of the sinner with the last breath of life. Speak, God is listening to you and will pardon you."

"My father," said the moribund, who died a moment later, "I don't believe in God."

The Evocateur

SHE was a very old lady, heavily perfumed and powdered, steeped in essences, so thin beneath the sad richness of her dresses and jewels that she represented well—frightfully well—the worldly skeleton, the elegant carcass that has never said its final word and which strikes poses even in annihilation.

Since she had lived alone in her old funeral town house, where the accumulated dust seemed a residuum of an ossuary, her life had continued, exactly similar—in reality—to the life of joys and triumphs that the former beauty had enjoyed for such a long time. No one, however, visited her except for rare heirs almost as old as her, whom she always received poorly. Often, she sent them away as soon as they arrived, under the pretext of the fallacious insanity that she was giving a great ball that very evening and that on such an occasion, the mistress of a house did not have time to waste chatting. She added: "I didn't invite you; these fêtes are not for people of your age."

Now, "that very evening," only a single person came—very discreetly—through the doors of the house, and the vast decorated drawing rooms were only illuminated by a dozen yellow candles, the lighting of a dance of the dead.

"Come in, Monsieur le Professeur, you're the only one lacking."

Monsieur le Professeur came in, bowing with the grace of a dancing-master, but hindered in his movements by an exceedingly red hat, which he tried to hide behind his back, and a lamentable violin-case, that unfailingly bumped into the batten of the door.

Rid of those accessories, he recommenced his salutations, advancing three paces, bowing slightly at the first two and profoundly at the third; then, one waits for the beautiful lady to offer her fingers to be kissed, and if she does not deign to do so, one retires modestly, hand on heart.

The beautiful lady never offered her hand to be kissed; Monsieur le Professeur therefore retired modestly, hand on heart, and, tuning his violin, asked: "Piano or violin, Madame la Marquise?"

Madame Marquise had them alternate; she preferred quadrilles on the violin and waltzes on the piano.

"Play us the Sicilian Quadrille," she said, negligently.

The evocateur played the introduction; the couples place themselves face to face and, on the keynote they advance, mingle, bow to one another—and between the murmur of rustling ball-gowns, a little pearly laugh rises and spills; the old marquise recognizes it: it is her own, sixty years ago.

A court ball, the first great ball at which she appeared, more emotional than the neophyte for whom the veil of Isis is to be torn. That evening she truly inaugurated her soul of a civilized virgin, conducting it to its baptism; hearing it said that one is "prettier than all the rest"—what benediction can compare to that one, and what benediction is as efficacious for insinuating into a gentle little heart amour and pity for her neighbor? How gladly she offered to "all the rest" the proud compassion of her happy gaze, her sovereign smile!

After the compliments, the declarations: exquisite phrases of romance, murmurs of sweet music, as sweet, in truth, as a melody by Marcailhou![1] Imagine that all those young men are affirming to you seriously that with a single word you could edify the palace of their felicity! Has anyone said as much to "another" since the commencement of the world, or a least since there have been court balls and gowns with low necklines? A single word: which? It's better to keep it quiet, for it is dangerous, and as soon as it is proffered, one is taken, which is much less amusing than taking oneself.

Meanwhile, Monsieur le Professeur has exhausted the figures of the Sicilian Quadrille; the shades stop with the final note of the gallop, and, disentangled, vanish.

"Monsieur le Professeur, play us the Waltz of the Willows now."

This one is almost grave. The initiate, become a hierophant, had enjoyed the mysteries and has shared the secrets with a chosen companion; but in order to be

---

[1] The composer Gatien Marcailhou d'Aymeric (1800-1855), famous in his day as a supplier of dance music, and a close friend of George Sand.

complete and truly a woman, it requires the certainty of the lie realized. It is only after having deceived that one attains the absolute blossoming, of true consciousness and liberty. The Waltz of the Willows was the prelude to that liberation, which was operated in three phases: a kiss on the shoulder, against which one does not protest; a request for rendezvous, to which one responds; and the rendezvous itself, a mere formality, since the adultery is already realized in intention.

Of those three phases, the most agreeable to remember was undoubtedly that of the kiss on the shoulder, an unexpected and new sensation—and then, the rest had been repeated so many times in the course of the years!

Once embarked on the Waltz of the Willows, the extravagant professor was able to navigate for entire hours; the boat descended slowly or furiously along an indefinite river that flowed into another river and never arrived, even after innumerable ramifications, at pouring its waves of harmony into the ocean of silence. The marquise was obliged to interrupt; she did so politely and almost with grace.

"Thank you, Monsieur le Professeur, the story is finished. Play us now, I beg you, the mazurka of the Last Amour."

Without hesitation, for his repertoire of out-of-date works was vast, the professional evocateur launched into the Last Amour, a "brilliant mazurka," and swinging his head in time, from one shoulder to the other, like a metronome. As soon as the third measure, he heard a little cry behind him, but he was not at all disconcerted by it; while continuing to sway in time, however, like an improved metronome, he darted suspicious glances over his shoulder and lent a very attentive ear to the progress of the emotion and the timbre of the mysterious little cries; gradually, he gathered his legs and detached himself from the stool, ready for the abrupt movement that might be necessary.

The marquise stood up and came to lean on the piano; she genuinely seemed moved, too emotional, and she looked at her professor of memories with terribly grateful eyes.

It was like a quest, quite futile, for improbable audacities; but the anxious evocateur hastened his final notes, suddenly stood up, bowed, picked up his violin case and, boldly putting on his hat, scornful of protocol, disappeared with an extreme rapidity.

Jose and Josettte

JOSE was very small. He went to school following sunken paths, leaping over gates, running alongside hedges, musing and robbing birds' nests, picking strawberries or hazelnuts, acidic berries or burnets. He was a meek and obedient child, but as soon as he was alone, he became as instinctive and as savage as a weasel or a shrew-mouse. He was not made to obey, any more than any other human creature, but a stare or a word tamed him. For as long as the impression subsisted he bowed down, humble under the will of the stronger.

One day, then, as he was going to school, twirling like a sling the satchel in which his mother had put a piece of bread and an apple, he encountered Josette, who was going to school, just like Jose.

Josette was weeping. She confessed that she had been punished and had fled in anger without eating her soup. She was hungry. Jose gave her his bread and his apple, and the child kissed him in order to thank him. She was no longer crying; she wanted to play. They played at hopping, walking on their knees and lying in the grass.

The schoolmaster, who was walking with the class, encountered them and said to them, severely: "You're two little guttersnipes. Is that how you play? It's necessary to play seriously. Why don't you play at who knows best the name of all the sub-prefectoires, or the names of the tributaries of the Loire, or the divisions of the metric system. You'll end up badly, I fear—he shook his head—and then, and then . . . what! Boy and girl! Little boys ought to go one way and little girls the other. Jose, go this way, and you, Josette, go that way."

Then, satisfied, he resumed the path to the school, but gradually, his hair stood up on his head, for he foresaw the unfortunate fate for which those children were destined.

He murmured: "Authority, discipline, geography, orthography . . . authority discipline . . ."

※

It was the parish fête. Dusk fell, candles were lit and there was dancing. Jose, who was eighteen, and Josette, who was fifteen, were there, in their best clothes, and at the first cries of the violin had enlaced one another under the eyes of families who were drinking cider and talking about old times, the future crop and taxes more terrible than hail.

When the first dance was finished, Josette, at a sign, went to join her mother

"Josette, my dear child, I beg you, don't dance any more with Jose. His father is ruined and he's nothing but a poor little farm boy. Don't let yourself be courted by that boy, for you can't marry him; we wouldn't consent to it. Money requires money. And you have money, my Josette, and Jose has not."

That evening, they did not dance together again.

❋

Jose's lot was drawn and he was a soldier. It was in that métier that he learned seriously what it is necessary to do and what it is necessary not to do. After four years he possessed a complete and respectable morality; he knew that there are two classes of men: superiors and inferiors, and that one recognizes the superiors by the good embroidered on their sleeves. Those notions were not to be useless to him when he emerged from the barracks, for in ordinary life, there are also two sorts of men: superiors and inferiors, those who work and those who watch others work. As he found that distinction quite natural, doubtless thanks to his instinctive philosophy, Jose worked.

Josette was not married. Her parents had lost everything in a bad lawsuit, and, a poor milkmaid, she went to milk the cows in the dew and thought that it was very sad not to have a lover.

Jose, on learning that news, was joyful. He confided his old amour to his father, and his plans.

"Marry Josette!" said the old peasant. "A girl who probably hasn't got three chemises and who makes her garters with a handful of hemp. You're not rich either, it's true, but you've made a little heritage; the wheat has rendered well this year, and I'll give you what you need to establish yourself when you bring me a daughter-in-law who isn't a servant. Money wants money, my son; it's necessary not to go against it."

※

Years passed. Jose lost his parents and, instead of an adorable woolen stocking, found debts. All courage and all labor were futile. Like mice, the men of law nibbled away the petty patrimony, and one day, Jose sold his house, took his staff and went away, as far as he could go, to seek his life, but as he went, life fled before him, and he walked so far and for such a long time that, having gone around the world, he found his field again by the roadside, where he had met Josette for the first time.

He put down his staff and, sitting on the edge of the ditch, he took a piece of bread and an apple out of his pocket. Before eating, he reflected sadly, so sadly that the apple and the piece of bread fell from his fingers.

It was cold, even sheltered from the wind; he pulled his great ragged cloak over his knees and wrapped his throat in the vast gray beard that had often frightened little girls.

As he was thinking about that, he heard shrill cries, and children who were coming back from school went by, exactly similar to those there had been more than sixty years ago. Suddenly, he understood the futility of everything and the abominable stupidity of life. He got up and brandished his empty satchel like a sling, and went around the field several times, as if hallucinated.

During the third circuit he fell into a big hole full of dry leaves. He stayed there, and as night was approaching he arranged himself in order to go to sleep.

However, an old beggar-woman arrived, moaning:

"Oh, old man, you can't stay there; that's my place. I sleep there every night. That hole is mine—mine, you hear?"

And as the old man obeyed, meekly, the old woman, after having examined him, said: "Where do you come from? I don't recognize you. What's your name?"

"People call me Old Jose."

"They call me Old Josette."

They looked at one another in silence. They remembered one another.

But they had suffered so much, and their hearts had become so dry, so similar to the dead leaves, that they could not think of anything to say.

Old Josette curled up in the hole like a wild beast, while Old Jose, picking up his staff, went away.

The Man who has Killed

A MAN similar to many men, he appeared to me for a long time to be a simple individual, with a very ordinary mechanism. I analyzed him and took him apart at a glance, but although he was not, in my opinion, one of those who are deceptive, he was one of those who hold the attention slightly, because of the pleasure one has in comparing them indefatigably with their neighbors. Without liking him, I had the esteem for him due to a good chess player; his cunning traps were classic, but so coldly planned and so far ahead that one always perceived too late, with the satisfied conclusion of a student, that one had been tricked within the rules, by procedures written in all the manuals.

We spent brief hours playing every evening, in a noisy café, troubled by the violent entrances of students accompanied by singular women. That made us raise our heads, but the chessboard remained in our eyes, and the bishops and knights extended a black and white curtain between our attention and the drunken smiles of the slender prostitutes.

None of them was known to me; they held out their hands to me as they passed by, careless of displeasing their lover of the evening, for the café, the center of a fraternal world, permitted familiarity. My friend—a friend I had never liked—was more often favored than I was by those little reminders and the little gloved hands, but the little hands, for which he never let go of the crenellations of the rooks, slid so rapidly through his fingers, and he savored the caress so slightly that, his eyes having remained obliquely lowered over the vision of the decisive move, he asked me a few minutes afterwards: "Who was that who said bonjour to me?"

Those distractions are common to all attentive and serious players, but it seemed to me that in him they took on a particular aspect, not of indifference, but of dread. When a woman stopped in front of him and spoke to him, it seemed that he became fearful; sometimes he went pale; often his fear ended up in a dissimulated anger, and an impertinence that was maladroit, or even stupid, rid him of the importunate woman. In truth, the women took no notice; they seemed to spare him; they drew away, after a rather affectionate word of reproach, and none bore any grudge

It was more than a year since we had begun to meet up at the café before my observations became more precise. I noticed—or, for it was so strange, I thought that I noticed—that on the rare occasions when there were no women in the café, my friend had a much greater freedom of mind and a more redoubtable precision of play. When it was full of women, and the enervating odor of females was redolent there, he was troubled and hesitant, and allowed himself to be beaten.

One evening, I said to him, after having examined the room: "I'll beat you today."

Obedient to my suggestion, he looked around, and then, in a very calm tone, he replied: "Yet, I believe you'll beat me today. I'm not on form, the contest will be more difficult for me. There are evenings when I feel inenbriated, by the dolorous intoxication that certain poisons provoke."

"To what do you attribute that?" I asked. "You don't have a nervous temperament."

After a hesitation, he said, slowly: "To what do I attribute that condition? To old things, a story, coincidences, memories . . . in sum, I can't and don't want to be more precise."

The final words were pronounced a little dryly, and I responded in the same fashion: "I've been indiscreet; I beg your pardon, all the more willingly because it's very indifferent to me." In order to palliate my interlocutor, I added: "The game is sufficient to my curiosity."

From that evening on my companion—the man I thought at first to be simple—gave me the pleasure of mystery, and I continued my observations passionately. That malady of sorts interested me greatly; I hoped to discover its cause and make my glory, for I had not read anything similar in descriptions of the strangest nervous maladies. Put in purely scientific terms, it was, in sum, the influence upon a man who appeared not to be very sensitive, of an accumulated female fluid.

Having found that explanation, I was not satisfied with it; however, it could not be completely absurd, for it is said that an assembly of men excites the nervousness of a woman, sometimes to the point of hysteria; in analogous conditions a man experiences a superabundance of male vitality; in the case I was studying—while watching from the shelter of my silent play—it was solely a matter of depression instead of excitation, less rather than more; instead of tipping slightly to the right, the balance was tipping toward the left, that was all.

My lame explanation temporarily admitted, it remained to find the primal cause; but as I did not know anything about my companion's life, as he had never made me any confidence, that final research appeared to me to be impossible, and I abandoned the solution. We continued to maneuver our knights, and I abstained, out of lassitude and ennui, from observations that were henceforth futile.

It happened one evening that a woman came into the café, of a rather mediocre beauty, but red-haired with a very white skin. She was alone and had the lamentable air of prostitutes who have trailed their skirts over the sidewalks for hours, in vain.

She sat down nearby; my friend raised his head and suddenly went so pale that I was afraid. At the same time, his hand, which was holding a conquering rook, fell back on the chessboard with such force that all the pieces were knocked over.

"Come on, I beg you," he said to me, in the voice of an invalid. "Let's go,"

He leaned tremulously in my arms. When he had taken a few steps, I heard him murmur very distinctly: "They all know, they all know . . . yes, I believe they know . . . it attracts them . . . the blood of their sisters . . . but that one, the one who sat down beside me, she loves me so much . . . that I'd be capable of killing her again."

I repeated: "Again?"

He looked at me. "Yes, again."

The Last Hour

HE was a somber and peevish man, and old age had ossified him. Prematurely aged, a slave to dolors and black ideas, he had already been gasping for years, castigating life, which he adored like a fleeting mistress, cajoling death, the syllable of which, pronounced, excited lamentable tremors in his memory and a supernatural horror in his soul.

All day long he wept, like a little child crouching in the chill of his underclothes—but he was only lamenting in order to be lamented, and left alone, he fell silent, going to sleep in the brutality of silence.

Before his wife and the kindness of his friends, the monotonous and poignant refrain formed a sort of indestructible foam over his white lips,

"Me, who deprived myself of everything in my youth, who only drank water and took undignified meals in the solitude of a poor room! Me, who passed by, proud and suspicious, with no more than a glance for the creatures of amour! Me, who always said to myself: 'Tomorrow you'll have the time! Tomorrow! What you disdain today with be returned to you a hundredfold—in your old age!" Me, who deprived myself of everything in order to live! Me, who never violated either the rules of hygiene or those of morality! Me, who was an integrally sealed citizen solely guided by the rule of the Useful! Me, me, me . . . !"

And in his verbal impotence, the mediocre old man, more sinister than a parricide and viler than a cesspit-emptier, spilled forth the grotesque rosary of *me, me, me* . . . ! For he had a singularly persistent egotistical personality and his imbecilic conscience was inveterate and indestructible.

At other times, with a senile indecency, he listed, in phrases intercut by coughing fits, the "opportunities" that he had once missed. His memory became pitiless and detailed the unique beauties of the hundred virgins of the brothel before whom his lust had been vanquished by his prudence. He remembered entering those houses with serious and blazing eyes, passing through, risking the gestures of the bawd, before the display of deviant breasts and excessive bellies, exchanging with stigmatized mouths filth as burning as caresses—and then shrugging his shoulders and fleeing toward the certainty of unhealthy dreams!

And at that moment, he regretted his economic prudence and fell into the abjection of regret for the honest loose woman celebrated in popular song.

Soon, however, that periodic eructation was forbidden to him; his tongue grew heavy and his brain was troubled; the frontal circumvolutions in which the wretched words formed by his tumefied lips were elaborated, turned into cat-food. Among the sounds that still gave evidence of the life of the sad paralytic, only vague obscene syllables could still be distinguished with the aid of careful attention.

The hour of the approaching trespass was manifest, and his maidservant, weary of late nights, installed next to the moribund a nun whose wimple and rosary signified that she would not get drunk during the calm of the night and would only become ecstatic by means of paternosters and hunger pangs.

The nun came in and, when the phials and the prescriptions had been explained to her, she perched on the edge of a chair, and from there soon fell to her knees, telling the gems of amour on her stout wooden rosary. She recited the supplications, invocations and glorifications in a low voice, and one might have thought that an invincible stall maintained her in the hard stance of the eternal prayers.

Sometimes, she turned her mild eyes, distracted by amour, toward the bed; more often, she raised them toward the ceiling, and certainly, through the ceiling, she saw the heavens, and the starry robe of the Virgin, and Jesus crowned like a king, leaning negligently on his cross, and angels absorbed in concertos, and, in sum, all the splendors of a court in which the diamonds are brilliant virtues on immaculate shoulders and candid breasts.

She was undoubtedly a woman about forty years old, but the silence and calm of her features rendered an exact appreciation difficult; in any case, she probably cared little about her age herself, since her lover was the one who rejuvenates at his whim all hearts and all faces, at the price of the virginity of the body, bestowing the eternity of the soul and the eternity of love. She had never thought of anything but doing her duty and fulfilling her obedience; she was naïve and indifferent, and if there had been tears in her life, those tears had become a placid stream always running limpid through the lilies of the valley. Her obedience, that night, was to spend ten hours in the bedroom of a dying man, and she was no more emotional than in spending other hours at the foot of the altar. She was here and she was there, in accordance with whether she was told to "go here" or "go there," and the certainty of no longer having any will gave elegance and grace to her actions.

Meanwhile, the moribund groaned, still ejaculating vague obscene syllables, appearing thus to vomiting fragments of his despicable soul of a lustful miser. Those excremental efforts lasted until morning, until the hour when the nun, running out of words, became drowsy on her knees, her forehead on a chair, like an invincible suppliant. At that moment, the dying man's eyes opened very wide, in order to drink in the familiar things that they were about to quit. They opened very wide, very wide, ready to envelop everything visible, determined to carry into infinity the supreme reflection of life—and those avid eyes, as they opened, as they turned, fell upon the torpid nun and stopped, as if on a prey.

That nun had the beautiful attitude of an amorous woman tearful and tired after a night of amour: that woman, alone, as if introduced for pleasure into the solitude of his bedroom . . . oh, that woman . . . !

He rediscovered phrases in order to murmur caresses, and gesture in order to extend his idle hands toward the vision, and strength in order to get up—and when the sleeper awoke it was to see at her knees a gasping specter lifting up her robe.

Emerence

MY aunts told me that they had found me a wife. I had arrived at the age at which a man who has no social ambition begins to be tired of being alone and having no one to tyrannize. The need for tyranny or commendation, or domination, is inveterate in the male; often, he only marries in order to be the lord and master, and if he is mistaken, if authority escapes him, it is a disappointment powerful enough to annihilate his will and debase his character forever. In order not to risk such an adventure, I intended to choose a woman who was docile without being servile, mild without being stupid, obedient without being a coward, and with sufficient beauty and grace to give me the sensation of possessing a luxurious, rare, dear animal difficult to replace. Horses had previously been my passion; I did not hope to find a woman as beautiful as a fine horse, but as I would enjoy her with one sense more, one beauty less would give me a greater pleasure.

I therefore listened to what my aunts said.

Old spinsters and twin sisters, they had brought me up with the respectful tenderness one has in some old families for the eldest son, the head of the family; from the age of twelve they had left me mastery, and would gladly have taken my orders had I not already had sufficient reason to refuse the responsibility that was offered to me. In any case, I loved them very much, and it was always agreeable for me to see in them prudent counselors, whose advice or desires I accepted deferentially.

"It's one of our distant cousins," my aunts told me—they almost always spoke in unison, and one only heard one voice—"Emerence de V***. She can please you in every way, for she has birth, fortune and beauty, if we've been correctly informed. You ought to go to see her."

"Under what pretext?"

"We'll arrange that. Wouldn't renewing family relationships, for example, be a convenient pretext? Monsieur de V***, we know, would be glad to receive you; he has very good hunts; he would retain you for a few days and you'd know whether Emerence is worthy of you. As for Madame de V***, she is ill, and does not occupy herself with anything."

Things were organized as my aunts wished, and I departed for the Château de Boisroger, expected by Monsieur de V***, who had sent me a most amiable invitation "as soon as he had been apprised of my desire to make the acquaintance of my old cousins."

It was rather a long way from my residence, but the railway would only take me to within five leagues of Boisroger and I decided to make the journey by carriage, which would not take much longer, having two good horses habituated to poor country roads. I departed at midday and at six o'clock I entered the courtyard of the château, stones still feudal that the hairy barbarians had not dishonored.

Monsieur de V*** was waiting on the perron; I arrived at the precise hour anticipated; he seemed delighted by that, congratulated me on such punctuality, and, as a countryman for whom animals are beloved and precious beings, he recommended my horses—which, in fact, were covered in foam—to the palfreyman.

"You've forced them somewhat," he said to me, "but I hope that you'll leave them time to rest."

When I had washed and changed, in a vast room with menacing tapestries depicting dragons and chimerical creatures, against which knights were fighting, armed with long lances like rays of starlight, Monsieur de V*** came to fetch me and we went down to the drawing room, where Madame de V***, as white in the face as in the hair, seemed to be dying in an armchair. Emerence, next to her, was poring over some tapestry-work, and three large tawny spaniels were curled up asleep under the high mantelpiece.

Madame de V*** responded to my compliments with a sickly smile and words so faint that I could not hear them.

When we came in, Emerence had stood up, putting aside her tapestry-work rather abruptly, and she extended her hand to me, while gazing at me with large brown eyes, very joyful but very mysterious. She was tall, pale, a trifle robust, full of life, but fatigued by an existence cloistered in the company of her infirm mother; she appeared to be slightly older that I had been told and did not have the appearance of a maiden. As she had pleased me at first glance, my heart was suddenly slightly constricted by that impression, and I wondered whether my good aunts might have been misinformed, and whether Emerence might be married. Then, blushing at my stupidity, for a marriage is the least unknown of circumstances, I concluded that, after all, a "virginal air" was quite indifferent and that a young woman of Emerence's beauty had no need of that vulgar spice to seduce me.

During dinner and the evening, while being as witty as possible, talking in my turn and even more—for a stranger must make himself known in order not to disoblige his guests—I observed Emerence and was soon conquered. Not only did I find her "worthy of me," as my aunts desired, but I wondered anxiously whether she would find me worthy of her. My ideas of authority and command lost their force, and, in order to win Emerence's amour, I would have obeyed the most absurd orders.

In order to distract Madam de V***, we played a game of *nain jaune*.[1] Emerence won a great many ivory chips and silver-plated medals, which her father redeemed with less rare coin, taken willingly from a

---

1 Nain jaune [yellow dwarf, named after the *conte* by Madame d'Aulnoy, one of the few tales she penned that ends tragically] is a card game, invented *circa* 1760, very popular in France in the early nineteenth century, especially with children, which also required a board with five compartments and a quantity of variously-colored chips. It is a game of chance from which players are eliminated one by one as they lose all their chips.

large deerskin purse; she was amused, she laughed, and she launched ambiguous remarks at me.

"Win in your turn, cousin! Win me, then!"

That was perhaps only ambiguous in my imagination, but I was glad to be able to flatter myself that I did not displease her.

When the candles were lit, Emerence said to me: "Every morning, cousin, I got to pick fruits from the espaliers before the sun has taken the sheen off them; only I can do that. Would you like to accompany me tomorrow morning? At seven o'clock, on the perron."

"But we were going hunting tomorrow," hazarded Monsieur de V***.

"You can go hunting another time," said Emerence. "He needs to see the espaliers. The peaches are as beautiful as angels."

Emerence had the last word, and I was delighted.

With a broad white hat over her hair and a large basket on her arm, shod in small clogs because of the dew, Emerence appeared on the perron at the same time as me and we set forth for the espaliers at the top of the park.

She no longer had her joyful attitude of the previous day; even paler, her eyes more profound, she seemed sad, and I thought I even saw her tremble.

When we had covered almost half the distance she said to me abruptly: "My cousin, you have come here for me, for me alone, and you have the intention of marrying me; I am aware of everything, and I'm very grateful to your aunts for having designated me to you, for I love your name, you're my relative and I would be glad to be your wife—but first, I have to tell you a story."

She reflected for a moment, and then went on: "Do I truly have the air of a maiden?"

I replied faintly, but with an indescribable emotion: "No, you have the air of a woman."

"I have the appearance because I am one," she said.

I did not know what to say; I followed her, my eyes lowered; I trembled in my turn.

"Hold the basket, without shaking it, like this."

She seemed calmer since her brutal confession. While collecting the peaches, she continued.

"Everyone knows the story except you and your aunts; if you haven't heard it now you would hear it eventually—and you would never forgive me. When you've heard it, you'll flee, after a few days accorded to politeness, and you won't give me another thought. I've made the experiment several times, and I'll continue for as long as my sad youth lasts. The story? It's stupid and vulgar. It was six years ago; I was eighteen; I was engaged to Monsieur de B***, who was my childhood friend; I loved him very much; we were allowed too much freedom; I had an absolute confidence in him; he amused me, went away and never returned. Two years later we learned that he was already married, in some colony or other. He has died since. However, I had a child—I still have one—a nameless child, whom I love, and who is my shame. That's the story of Emerence de V***, who is picking peaches with her cousin for the first and last time."

"You're mistaken, Emerence," I said, violently. "I'm rich enough not to be accused of trafficking; I'm richer than you; I'll efface your shame and you'll make my joy. Give me your hand."

Emerence, who was standing in front of me, started weeping silently; two large tears trickled on to her pale cheeks. I let her weep; she wept abundantly; the tears that were running down her pale cheeks had obstructed her heart for too long; she needed to weep.

Then she looked at me with the anxiety of someone resuscitated, and her large brown eyes asked me whether I too had lied, but I drew nearer to her and I said: "Since we're betrothed, Emerence, allow me to kiss your hands."

The Burned Château

WHEN the dishes were cleared, all three of them had remained around the table, but they said little, like people whose ideas are rare and who, always repeating the same things, have the instinct of putting intervals between their remarks.

Monsieur de Brunon was drinking brandy from a silver goblet; he poured it from an old crystal decanter sculpted and gilded, which he lifted up to eye level every time he filled his cup, making it shine in the lamplight. One divined that he loved the decanter for the brandy that sparkled within the sculpted and gilded glass, and the brandy for the beauty of the decanter and the memories of ancient joys imprisoned there, which might be about to emerge with the last glass and the last spark.

He drank like that every evening, while his daughter Danielle read some mediocre story or embroidered the corner of a handkerchief. She too was gilded; as she always inclined her head over her reading or her needlework, nothing was seen of her head but blonde hair; when her father thought about her, he evoked her blonde hair, and nothing but the blonde hair, for the young woman's face troubled him, hard and cold, with something in the eyes similar to the implacable spirit asleep in brandy decanters.

Since the death of Madame de Brunon, whose fantasies of vanity had ruined the household, the two of them had lived alone in a painful dignity, attentive to maintaining the conduct and costume required by their name and their estate. Careful above all of appearances, their skill was so great that they even deceived their domestics and their notary.

Twice a year, the hard and cold Danielle absented herself, taking a large old trunk constellated with brass nails, and when she came back her first words were a number, pronounced in a curt voice.

In the epoch when Baudoin de B*** arrived, awaited for years, at the Château de Brunon, Danielle did not have a single ring left on her fingers; when she embroidered, she hid her left hand beneath the piece of muslin. Cold and hard as she was, her father saw her weeping one day, and looking at her long white naked hands. That day, Monsieur de Brunon only drank half his decanter of brandy.

"I've never forgotten you, Danielle," Baudoin said, when Monsieur de Brunon, having emptied his last glass, went to sleep. "Here, still on my little finger, is the little ring that I stole from you, swearing to come back and return it to you. Give me your hand."

Danielle held out her long white bare hand.

"You don't wear a ring any longer?"

"No, I was waiting for you to return it to me."

Danielle was almost emotional. Those pretty childish gestures of sentiment softened her metal heart a little. For a few hours, her soul became as young as her face again, and her eyes became mild to the point of tenderness.

Quite astonished, he perceived that change in her condition.

"If I were as rich as before, Baudoin, I would be as amiable and as good as before. But I know that I have become wicked, that I have become hard and cold—and that is irreparable."

Then she told Baudoin the whole truth. He was not very profoundly touched by it, for his was a simple and disinterested heart. He loved Danielle, with an amour that had not been diminished by the revelation of her poverty, and, taking her long white bare hands, despoiled of their rings, he kissed them one after the other, and said: "I'll keep them, all white, bare and pure."

"Yes, Baudoin," Damielle repeated, "all poor, poor, poor."

"Poor!" exclaimed Monsieur de Brunon, suddenly, awakened by the sad syllables that haunted his sleep. He sat up and extended his hand toward the gilded decanter. "It's empty, my child; will you go fill it for me?"

Danielle got up, took the decanter, and went to lift up a flap of tapestry, behind which an oak cask was asleep, full of dreams and illusions: an oak cask from which, no doubt, the magic word was about to emerge that liberates the golden dragon, the master and guardian of human joy.

When the decanter was on the table, Monsieur de Brunon, having made it shine, filled a goblet therefrom, and said: "It's more beautiful than ever. It's resplendent; Danielle, I believe that this time it's going to reveal its secret. Drink with me, Baudoin."

Baudoin yielded, and dank a few glasses of brandy.

"Poor!" repeated Monsieur de Brunon. "And to think that this old château, haunted by the dead, is insured for . . . enormous sums. What sum, Danielle? And may it never burn."

"Don't say that, father. Matter, which is inert, obeys speech, which is alive. This château will burn one day. When? No one knows yet. Drink another glass of this brandy, Baudoin; perhaps it will tell you its secret—the secret that it has always refused my father."

And Baudoin drank another glass of brandy.

※

A few hours later, Monsieur de Brunon, his daughter and Baudoin, enveloped in blankets, were huddled in the straw of a farm shed, while the high and beautiful flames writhed harmoniously, yellow and red, above the pyre predicted by Danielle. Monsieur de Brunon was weeping, frightened by the magical realization of his abominable dream. Baudoin, semi-conscious, was breathing heavily, lying on his back, his fingers agitated by nervous gestures. Danielle, on her knees, appeared to be praying; her long white hands, on which a single ring glittered, were joined, and her face, illuminated by the conflagration, was resplendent, as if supernatural.

Baudoin, almost delirious, uttered vague words; she ran to him then and kissed him on the mouth.

"Shut up, shut up!" she murmured. "Your speech belongs to me. Now we're united by a cement stronger than amour."

"Crime," said Baudoin.

"Shut up; I love you."

She wrapped Baudoin's docile arms around her neck.

His lips pressing Danielle's lips, he thought, obscurely: *I'm enslaved by this woman forever.*

The Collector

HE was a silent, passionate man, whose life had but one goal. A collector, but exclusive and cruel, endowed with the eyes of a raptor and feline hands, he had a unique way of looking at the object of his covetousness and a unique fashion of gripping it: the eye of a hawk and the thrust of a cat's paw. His passion was prints. He saw them through cardboard boxes, through the binding of albums, through the doors of cupboards, and when the box or cupboard was opened for him he advanced his hand with a curt gesture and took them.

The print merchants loved him, for he lacked the kind of shrewdness by which a collector veils beneath indifference, or even disdain, the tremor of his desire. With him, there was little haggling; his eyes and hands said too clearly: *I want that, I want it, I want it*—and the price proffered, he paid, and took it away.

His profession was barely suspected; he was thought—true, it was known when he died—to be the chief of a bureau in a ministry, and personally rich as well, but to any question or allusion he remained mute.

His name, which would have permitted anyone curious to make enquiries, was unknown. He never had his purchases sent to his domicile. The prints that he bought went immediately into an enormous box that awaited him in a carriage, and he soon disappeared, hardly having opened his mouth.

Between themselves, the print merchants and salesmen called him Monsieur Collector, and that name seemed to suit him essentially. He was, in appearance, the type specimen of the egotistical and grim collector, and nothing more: the model, perhaps abominable, but complete and perfect, of the solitary player, the man whose fornication is lavished on inert matter, endowed with the only life that gives rise to his desire. Monsieur Collector was that, but also something more—and something very different.

In reality, the man's passion was the hatred of art; he only bought prints in order to torture them, and in them to torture art and all artists. His gynaeceum was a torture chamber; he tormented once a week, on Sunday.

On that day, Monsieur Collector did not go out. On that day, he did not eat or drink; he put Dürer on the rack and Holbein on the wheel.

Little weekly vacations! Naturally, he thought about it all week long. His colleagues made plans for that day of liberty the mediocrity of which surprised him; the least ridiculous of those plans seemed to him to be infantile, and he felt, above all, a great pity for an old deputy, entirely white-haired, who dreamed about verdure, birds and fried fish, and who did not blush to confess thus the grotesque secret of his sexagenarian heart. Others spoke about their children, their wives, their mistresses, and those preoccupations Monsieur Collector found ludicrous; he sometimes shrugged his shoulders and added: "Personally, on Sundays, I sort out my prints."

And on Sundays, he sorted out his prints.

Taking all the week's acquisitions from the box, he set them out on a large table and contemplated them at length, enjoying their beauty. That was the amorous phase. Ecstasized by the ensemble, he went on to the details, delighting in the subtle radiance with which Rembrandt transpierces shadows, the powerful contours by which Dürer models the rumps of his horses and his women, and the charity of line with which Callot envelops the fantasy of his beggars and matadors; he intoxicated himself with beautiful curves and bold models; he enjoyed the finesse of shading, the softness of gleams, the profound intensity of blackness: forms whose young grace reawakens the desire to be young; maturities and plenitudes that inspire serious amours; troubling lives made of a little ink thrown on to a piece of paper.

After the amour, not abruptly but by virtue of a slow degradation of sentiments, Monsieur Collector experienced envy, and his mediocrity was gradually exasperated, and grew to the extent of hatred. His envy was complex; he envied simultaneously the genius of the artists and the beauty of their works, but above all, he was saddened by the glory of the masters, and, before the radiance of foreheads full of thought and eyes full of amour, he felt more obscure and colder.

The hatred surged forth; his lips curled back over clenched teeth, his fists closed convulsively, his heart beat faster, a prelude to crime. Then, calmed by that crisis, he got up and prepared the executions.

An easel,[1] an inkwell and a brush: that apparatus was sufficient for the executioner.

He placed a Dürer on the easel, and slowly, with the precautions of a scrupulous artist, he passed over the noble print a precise black stripe, then another, and then yet another, and from time to time he stepped back in order to see the lamentable effect of the indelible stains. Often—as it became possible to judge later—the torturer lost his sang-froid, and then there was a furious daubing, drunken outrages, a hideous massacre of sweeps, stains, stripes, to such an extent that people, frightened by such a terrible sadism, would have taken Monsieur Collector for a madman.

He was not mad—unless hatred of art is a sign of madness; but who would dare to sustain such a subversive opinion?

Monsieur Collector, therefore, simply had a hatred of art, and, as a friend of logic, he expressed that hatred as best he could and by the clearest, the most undeniably significant means.

The print thoroughly spoiled, and forever—for Monsieur Collector employed black ink of an excep-

---

1 It is significant, in the context of this story, that the French word *chevalet*, here translated as easel, can also mean a torturer's rack, as rendered in translation earlier in the text.

tional quality—he allowed it to dry, and then filed it separately in a series of boxes in which, uniformly, the word *Cemetery* was inscribed; the executioner buried his victims himself.

On Monsieur Collector's death, an inventory was made of his victims; there were thousands of them, and they had all been beautiful. Here and there, under the sinister stains, the knee of a horse, the shoulder of a woman or a broken sunbeam was visible: a gaze of light weeping in the night . . .

Monsieur Collector hated Art.

The End of the Walk

ARAMAN was not an ordinary walker, one of those who stroll, stopping at a window-display, taking an interest in an accident, turning round to follow with a vaguely concupiscent eye a rapid female passer-by cleaving through the crowd like a trout in the shadow of flowing water. He walked methodically, in accordance with principles elaborated once and for all; he walked rationally, for reasons of hygiene—by prescription, in sum. Those quotidian ambulations did not give him any pleasure, and many a time, during the three regulation hours, he took out his watch anxiously. Nevertheless, he was punctual; every afternoon, in the worst weather, even snow, he went out and set forth—toward nothing, at random, the faithful slave of the great goddess, for one who has dethroned Isis: Hygeia.

Marching, but above all on broad roads, along the exterior boulevards, empty of sordid exhalations, across deserts such as the Esplanade, amid the sinister boscage of the Champ de Mars, he went further, over the fortifications, along the highways, all the way to the woods.

After three weeks of that hard regime he had attained the state that the Greek philosophers called ataraxia: a complete indifference to anything that one might encounter in the course of a walk, from a tottering baby to a drunken clergyman, who seems to have acquired, by way of alcohol, a new dignity, a new human condition. Then, his excursions became increasingly difficult, and he foresaw the day when the determining motivation would be lacking, when he would become similar to the English poet Thomson,[1] who, found in bed at five o'clock in the afternoon, replied to his surprised and scandalized friend: "But I can't see any reason to get up."

That was when an idea of genius saved him.

There is an infallible means to making even an indolent or weary horse walk faster, and that is to put it behind a meritorious trotter; the idle creature, spurred by vanity or drawn by a master's authority, follows the heels of the courage that is showing it the way.

Araman adopted that system. He harnessed himself to march, step for step, in the wake of . . . a woman.

Women achieve, without drawing breath, without even hesitating for the most enticing spectacle, veritable voyages through Paris. As they have the precious faculty of not seeing, of not observing, entirely absorbed and hypnotized by the objective pursued, they are capable of marching indefinitely, so to speak, and accomplish-

---

[1] This incident was related of the poet James Thomson (1700-1748), author of "The Castle of Indolence" (1748), although he was Scottish, not English, and the original version of the anecdote only has him being found in bed at noon.

ing, almost without perceiving it, courses that would intimidate Ahasuerus.

So Araman started following women.

He chose one of those who seemed to have departed resolutely, ballasted for a serious crossing, which he recognized by the assured and definitive fashion in which they lifted up their skirts, the precise, rhythmic thrust of their heels and the little bag that they clutched more amorously to their hip, by something definitive, determined and simultaneously grave.

The majority of those female journeys ended with an abrupt flight through a coaching entrance, a disappearance so sudden that the slightest distraction enabled him to lose sight of them, like madcap swallows. He learned that no woman ever goes out without a precise goal, for pleasure; they always know where they are going, and nothing can draw them away from their path when they have resolved not to be distracted. A woman, he was soon assured, is a frightfully practical being, doubtless very capable of losing her way, but incapable of setting forth for the pleasure of exercising her pretty legs.

In following one of those women one is not risking either going astray or any obligation to make futile halts; they go straight ahead, often by the longest route, but forcefully, without stopping, as if pushed by a demon or attracted by a magnet—which can only be a lover.

Araman, on the other hand, had no other goal but to follow her; he played the role of the bad horse, and played it with a perfect discretion, careful not to disturb one of those agreeable sinners, those petty adulteresses.

Now, it happened that one of those agile lovers, in contradiction to the behavior of her sisters, turned her head, perceived a follower, slowed down, and made Araman understand, by a certain attitude, certain movements of her skirts and abrupt halts—by an entire discreet but evident play—that she consented to cut her journey in two and linger, for an appropriate time, in some improvised station. At least, Araman thought so, and, following the unknown woman, he ventured into a strange house, black, bleak, cold and mute, which resembled the hostelry of Death.

As soon as he went in, he was afraid; the breath of cellars filled the courtyard, where yellow grass surrounded disjointed paving-stones. The windows were only ornamented with cracked or broken panes, replaced with wooden boards, dusters or old newspapers; purulence was oozing from the walls, and at intervals, loosened by damp, flakes of plaster fell, crushed in the mud of a saline stream that ran alongside the walls. Araman raised his head and was very surprised to see that the sixth and last floor appeared to be resplendent with frescoes and decorations, brightened by sumptuous stained glass that the sun seemed to be caressing with joy and tenderness, and with the respect that beauty inspires even in the Sun.

The click of a heel made him lower his eyes; the unknown woman was waiting for him impatiently

He caught up with her and went into a frightful black and sticky spiral staircase that might, he thought, have been the interior staircase of a leprosarium.

He went up, and on the sixth floor there was the dazzle of a paradise: cedar-wood steps, carpet as profound as stable-litter, tapestries in which the crazed eyes of goblins and undines, aegipans and sirens, fays and angels smiled in crimson and gold.

No domestic staff: the door-curtains lifted of their own accord and doors opened as soon as a hand was advanced. Following the unknown woman, he traversed several rooms, each rich with a different richness: here, divine marbles; there angelic paintings; elsewhere the most sumptuous fabrics and the most adorable trivia. At the end, he found a sort of sanctuary, but with no other altar than a harmonious heap of cushions.

Although he had not made any gesture, his garments were suddenly transformed into a beautiful robe of violet silk, under which he as naked. He opened the robe and mirrors told him that he was handsome, with a superhuman beauty, astral and almost transparent. At the same moment, the unknown woman, who had been invisible for a few seconds, surged forth before him in all the splendor of a hallucinatory nudity. From head to foot her skin was smoother than ivory, and no imprudent stain interrupted its harmony. As he contemplated her, she approached him, and he soon sensed beneath his hands the freshness of two quivering shoulders.

Their joys were accomplished in silence, and were infinite.

Having enjoyed, without astonishment, so many unexpected sensualities, Araman went to sleep—and woke up in the street.

※

"I shouldn't have touched her," he said, later. "I felt, when my hands brushed her shoulders, even in the midst of an indescribable pleasure, I know not what disappointment in discovering by that contact an exceptional, perhaps unique flesh—yes, perhaps unique—but the flesh, in sum, of a woman, not entirely illusory."

He added: "It has been given to me—me, just anyone—to attain the Ideal, through what putrefaction! I've touched her, held her in my arms, kissed her with my lips, enjoyed her, and I've seen—the eyes of the Ideal were a mirror—I've seen in her eyes my own eyes, resplendent, and then dying of voluptuousness ... then ..."

And he also said: "I should have got down on my knees; I should have stayed on my knees, contemplating."

The Innocent Siren

LIONEL PAPPE gazed at absurd old engravings scorned by the men of today, and he visited with joy the landscapes inscribed in pale ink on frail yellow paper.

His voyage took him to an utterly bare isle, the shore of which was strewn with bones that seemed to have been brought there by the waves, pebbles rolled by the anger of the waves and the irony of the winds. In spite of that ugliness and the soil devoid of trees, grass and moss, the isle was pleasant and easy on the eye, because of a roseate vapor that enveloped it with a charm and gave sad skulls the appearance of large dying flowers.

Having more than one country to travel, Lionel Pappe was about to turn the page, already distracted by another desire, when a concert of voices and violins rose from the shores of the bare and roseate isle. Perched on the rock, three beautiful birds with women's faces were singing in an unknown language about infinitely sweet things, and in the water, three ambiguous beings, women in the head and upper body, were accompanying on nacreous violins the amorous song of the three beautiful birds.

Recognizing the sirens, Lionel Pappe smiled with a great deal of disdain, and began to make a critique, aloud, of that vain performance. He recognized the siren-bird genre; Homer had mentioned them, and he had seen a portrait in the Louvre of those singular creatures, sculpted for the ornament of an obscure bas-relief.

"The others are the classic monsters . . . but why are they playing the violin? The violin is not archeological. I have made a very ridiculous voyage this morning.

"My child," Lionel Pappe repeated to a young woman who had entered discreetly, a big blonde schoolgirl with bright eyes, almost as beautiful as the pale images inscribed on the pale yellow paper, "I have made a very ridiculous voyage this morning."

And the good professor, as a prologue to his lesson, recounted his excursion to the sad and roseate island.

"Yes, you're truly a good professor, Monsieur Pappe; you teach me things that aren't written either in books or on papyrus, nor on metal or marble. So you've seen sirens playing the violin?"

"I've seen that," replied Lionel Pappe, "and although ridiculous, I deem it disquieting."

"Because it isn't archeological?"

"Indeed, because it isn't archeological."

"I suppose," said the big schoolgirl with the bright eyes, "that you've never been afraid of sirens?"

"Why would I be afraid of sirens?"

"Because they're women."

"And you think, my child, that I'm afraid of women?"

"You ought to be afraid of things that are illogical, and women are illogical. They play the violin inappropriately; for grave and archeological men, they're ridiculous—like your sirens."

Lionel Pappe was surprised to hear such a speech. He looked at his pupil and perceived that he had before him a big schoolgirl with bright eyes, who was shaking her long curly hair proudly, and whose bosom was lifted up anxiously by tempestuous waves that were swelling and did not know where they were going to break. He was a prudent man, although very much a dreamer, and since he had been giving lessons to young girls he had never had the spectacle of such a metamorphosis. He treated his pupils as pupils, and none had yet reared up like this, ingenuously admitting the covetousness of his sex—and truly, he was afraid.

Lowering his eyes, he said, slowly: "My child, we'll continue our reading. Act three, scene eight."

"Monsieur Pappe," said the big schoolgirl, as if she had not heard, "what color are violin strings? Red, aren't they?"

"Yes," replied Lionel Pappe, obligingly. "A beautiful crimson. Now . . ."

"A crimson as bloody as this, as brightly red against the whiteness of nacre?"

As she spoke, she had opened her bodice, showing a red line on her left breast, very bright, on which blood pearled when she applied her hand to it, in a tragic manner.

"Monsieur Pappe, I tried to kill myself yesterday. Amorous chagrin? Not at all. I'm virginal in body and heart and I don't desire any lips—and can you believe that if I desired lips, they would turn away from mine? If I'd had an amour or caprice I'd have satisfied it. No, I wanted to kill myself precisely because I had no amour, nor desire, and hardly any curiosity, so faint that it wasn't worth the trouble of taking my dress off—my absurd big schoolgirl's black dress, shiny on the hip because of the bag I take to school. I wanted to kill myself out of ennui, I wanted to kill myself out of disgust for the miserable life that is destined for me. I wanted to kill myself out of hatred for the imbecilic books that have been imposed on my poor virginal intelligence, out of horror for the mental humiliation in which the rules maintain me under their barbaric feet. I wanted to kill myself because I believed that I could only liberate myself by consenting to forfeit my very liberty, because I believed that my beauty could only be affirmed by giving itself as a slave to a master—and because I don't want to give myself to a master. To all, yes; to one alone, no! I wanted to kill myself, and I was a coward—like a woman! When I felt the sting of the blade, my hand weakened, the tip of the weapon lifted, drawing along the skin that it skimmed this crimson thread. I'd like the scar always to remain vivid and red; that will remind me eternally of the moment when death enabled me understand life. I want to live. I'm only a woman; metaphysics doesn't attain me; I'm outside the range of its arrows, and it seems to me that I'd understand very well if anyone wanted to inform my flesh."

With a hysterical laugh, leaning toward Lionel Pappe, she said: "That's the crimson thread that is the red string of the sirens' violin."

"Child," said Lionel Pappe, "why seek excuses for desire? Let your flesh sing like the sirens' violin; never reflect about yourself, or solid images, or life, or death—and never come back here, for you'd be ashamed, innocent siren, of the victim of your song of love."

But the siren wept, and Lionel Pappe knew that tears are as salty as the sea in which the sirens swim.

Dialogue Between Harvede and a Shade

HARVEDE went back toward the hearth, where the soul of a forest was burning in flames of gold and azure. Huddled there, under a hedge of furs and cushions, he was still cold.

I have a chill in my soul, he thought.

He felt, along the length of his body from his forehead to his ankles, zones of ice that were cutting him up into five or six anxious and irritated Harvedes. He was brought tea, alcohol and perfumes; then the isothermic bands relaxed, and the icy serpents warmed up, to coil like fiery serpents.

I'm not as cold, he thought.

Unity was recomposed. Having become homogenous again, Harvede stirred and stretched—and then he desired.

Suddenly, that desire had come to him like an apparition, like a jet of sunlight.

"I'd like a blonde woman, a slave, a gentle creature ready to extend a neck with capricious arabesques and lattices . . ."

He was dreaming so forcefully that a malaise oppressed his heart, for he had rediscovered himself alongside the river whence came three beautiful young women, still naked from having undressed under the sun; their hair was suggestive of jets of water. One of them was *that* one, the one with the welcoming name; she only laughed in smiles, and her eyes remained as grave as the reflections of the profound and gentle river.

I'm no longer cold, Harvede thought.

He also thought: *It's too impossible. I don't like the absurd. I'd like to go to sleep.*

He had narcotics brought to him; and he went to sleep.

It was that moment that a voice chose to say, aloud: "Here I am, Harvede."

"You?"

"I loved you, and I love you still."

"You?"

"Me, the same, and henceforth immutable."

"You doubtless have no name, for I never heard you named—and I know many names; I know more names than are written in books and on parchments."

"If I have no name for you, I'll deny for all the others the name that I might have. After all, I am the one you know, the one who has eyes as grave and mild as the reflection of the river, one of the three, the one that cannot laugh, but who is able to smile."

"I haven't seen you for twenty years," said Harvede, "but you haven't changed. I thought you were dead. When I don't see people, I think they're dead. You're beautiful."

"Perhaps that's because I'm dead," said the shade,
"You're frightening me."

"Perhaps that's because I love you," said the shade.

"If you loved me," said Harvede, "it was necessary to give me your mouth and your breasts on the day when you emerged from the water."

"It was necessary to take them," said the shade. Having said that, the shade turned her head, and then went on: "You almost made me laugh—me, who can't laugh."

"Why?" asked Harvede.

"Because you speak hypocritically, like a dupe. Admit it, and I'll speak like you: you've taken me . . . in a dream."

"No, in desire only. In those days of my youth, I didn't dream, I lived. Perhaps I've mistaken another for you."

"Well, that's the same thing."

"You're not extravagant," said Harvede

"You want me, then?" said the shade.

"No," said Harvede.

"Am I no longer beautiful, then? You found me beautiful when I appeared."

"You are beautiful, since you're blonde—but you're only a shade."

"Child," said the shade, "look! I have only to open my shroud, like a robe of amour, for you to ask to kiss my skin of gem salt. Do I not shine like a diamond, with all the nuances of life and amour. It's said that I emerge from the water; I'm fresh and ardent; I bleed when I'm pricked; I burn when I'm touched—I burn and I melt. Truly, you don't desire me?"

"No, I don't desire you. You fled me when I was new to ruses; you fled me after having gazed at me and smiled at me . . ."

"I didn't flee you; I walked on, and you didn't follow me . . ."

"Yes, I was too young . . . but now, no. I know what you are now."

"You don't know. Take my hand."

Harvede took her hand.

"Is that consoling?" the shade asked. She continued: "Put your lips on my shoulder."

Harvede put his lips on her shoulder.

"Is that sad? Are my hands real? Is my flesh real? Touch my entire body. I'm real, I'm you, I'm immortal. Oh, my love, accept the pleasure that I bring you, therefore."

Harvede replied, a little tremulously: "I accept the pleasure that you bring me, but I accept it involuntarily. I'm accepting it because your odor is stifling my will."

"Be happy in peace, friend; I really am the one you desire."

"I don't know any longer."

"Yes, you persist in believing that I'm only a shade. I'm so alive, my dear, that I can give you death."

The voice of the shade became bitter and cruel, while Harvede forgot his conscience.

"You've kissed my shoulder. You've made a mistake. Why trust me? My skin of gem salt is poisonous. It's true that I'm Desire, the irresistible Desire, the absence of which afflicts and the presence of which sickens. Come on, let's love one another."

"Where are you taking me?"

"I love you; I'm all yours."

"I'm dying."

"How do you like death?"

"Delectable. Come back to see me, child."

"Child, we'll no longer be apart."

Harvede trembled more forcefully, and said: "I'm frightened; I really am dying."

"Really?" asked the shade.

"Let me go!"

The shadow loosened her hands, already tenacious.

"Yes, I'll let you go. You make me feel pity; you don't know how to die."

A PARTIAL LIST OF SNUGGLY BOOKS

G. ALBERT AURIER *Elsewhere and Other Stories*
S. HENRY BERTHOUD *Misanthropic Tales*
LÉON BLOY *The Tarantulas' Parlor and Other Unkind Tales*
ÉLÉMIR BOURGES *The Twilight of the Gods*
JAMES CHAMPAGNE *Harlem Smoke*
FÉLICIEN CHAMPSAUR *The Latin Orgy*
FÉLICIEN CHAMPSAUR
   The Emerald Princess and Other Decadent Fantasies
BRENDAN CONNELL *Clark*
BRENDAN CONNELL *Unofficial History of Pi Wei*
ADOLFO COUVE *When I Think of My Missing Head*
QUENTIN S. CRISP *Graves*
QUENTIN S. CRISP *Rule Dementia!*
LADY DILKE *The Outcast Spirit and Other Stories*
CATHERINE DOUSTEYSSIER-KHOZE *The Beauty of the Death Cap*
BERIT ELLINGSEN *Now We Can See the Moon*
BERIT ELLINGSEN *Vessel and Solsvart*
EDMOND AND JULES DE GONCOURT *Manette Salomon*
GUIDO GOZZANO *Alcina and Other Stories*
RHYS HUGHES *Cloud Farming in Wales*
J.-K. HUYSMANS *Knapsacks*
COLIN INSOLE *Valerie and Other Stories*
JUSTIN ISIS *Pleasant Tales II*
JUSTIN ISIS (editor) *Marked to Die: A Tribute to Mark Samuels*
VICTOR JOLY *The Unknown Collaborator and Other Legendary Tales*
BERNARD LAZARE *The Mirror of Legends*
BERNARD LAZARE *The Torch-Bearers*
MAURICE LEVEL *The Shadow*
JEAN LORRAIN *Errant Vice*
JEAN LORRAIN *Masks in the Tapestry*
JEAN LORRAIN *Nightmares of an Ether-Drinker*
JEAN LORRAIN *The Soul-Drinker and Other Decadent Fantasies*

ARTHUR MACHEN *N*
ARTHUR MACHEN *Ornaments in Jade*
CAMILLE MAUCLAIR *The Frail Soul and Other Stories*
CATULLE MENDÈS *Bluebirds*
CATULLE MENDÈS *To Read in the Bath*
EPHRAÏM MIKHAËL *Halyartes and Other Poems in Prose*
LUIS DE MIRANDA *Who Killed the Poet?*
OCTAVE MIRBEAU *The Death of Balzac*
CHARLES MORICE *Babels, Balloons and Innocent Eyes*
DAMIAN MURPHY *Daughters of Apostasy*
DAMIAN MURPHY *The Star of Gnosia*
KRISTINE ONG MUSLIM *Butterfly Dream*
YARROW PAISLEY *Mendicant City*
URSULA PFLUG *Down From*
JEAN RICHEPIN *The Bull-Man and the Grasshopper*
DAVID RIX *A Blast of Hunters*
FREDERICK ROLFE (BARON CORVO) *Amico di Sandro*
FREDERICK ROLFE (BARON CORVO)
  An Ossuary of the North Lagoon and Other Stories
JASON ROLFE *An Archive of Human Nonsense*
BRIAN STABLEFORD *Spirits of the Vasty Deep*
BRIAN STABLEFORD (editor)
  Decadence and Symbolism: A Showcase Anthology
COUNT ERIC STENBOCK *Love, Sleep & Dreams*
COUNT ERIC STENBOCK *Myrtle, Rue and Cypress*
COUNT ERIC STENBOCK *Studies of Death*
DOUGLAS THOMPSON *The Fallen West*
TOADHOUSE *Gone Fishing with Samy Rosenstock*
JANE DE LA VAUDÈRE *The Demi-Sexes and The Androgynes*
JANE DE LA VAUDÈRE *The Double Star and Other Occult Fantasies*
JANE DE LA VAUDÈRE *The Mystery of Kama and Brahma's Courtesans*
JANE DE LA VAUDÈRE *Syta's Harem and Pharaoh's Lover*
AUGUSTE VILLIERS DE L'ISLE-ADAM *Isis*
RENÉE VIVIEN *Lilith's Legacy*